THE 7 BIGGEST MISTAKES TRUSTEES MAKE

And How to Avoid Them

THE 7 BIGGEST MISTAKES TRUSTEES MAKE

And How to Avoid Them

Sandeep Varma

S & N Publishing

San Diego

First Printing 2007

Cover design by Mayapriya Long, *Bookwrights*
Interior design by Christopher Glenn
Printed in the United States of America

ISBN 10: 0-9795593-0-8
ISBN 13: 978-0-9795593-0-3

For more information, contact the publisher:

Sandeep Varma, *LPL Financial Advisor*
Advanced Trustee Strategies Financial
1 (888) 446-8275
www.atsfinancial.com

Contents

For Appendices A-D, go to:
www.sevenbiggestmistakes.com/appendices

Dedication

This book is dedicated, with gratitude and affection to my loving, patient, and accomplished wife — Nisha, and our precious children Ashni, Smita, and Sanjeev. Over the years Nisha has managed to juggle the kids, the office, and this book. Without her patience and dedicated involvement, this book, which I hope will help so many, would have never been possible.

Sound Familiar?

Introduction

I decided to write this book to help individuals accomplish their long-term financial goals successfully. Working with people as a financial professional, I learn a great deal about human nature. I have seen true goodness in people, but I have also seen greed that rips families apart—to where multiple siblings consider themselves each an only child. My job as a financial advisor is to provide individuals with good financial advice. With today's information society, there are many places to look for advice. For instance, the Internet can be a good source of information; but how reliable is it? When it comes to investing, there is too much information out there. It scares people off, and they procrastinate. When considering obstacles to achieving your financial goals, procrastination is just as bad as taxes and inflation.

Throughout my years, I have been involved with many families in their estate planning and have been successful in almost every case. I help set goals and show how to achieve them. I look at when a couple wants to retire and how much they need to accumulate to be able to do this. I look at other goals for them along the way, such as a house or college education for their children. I also help set up their estate in a trust so that, when they are gone, their heirs would get all their hard-earned money.

I always try to minimize what Uncle Sam collects, in order to benefit the family the most. As a financial advisor, I want to help my clients make decisions about investing so that they can enjoy their financial success.

This book is written for someone who sees the importance of managing money but might not have much knowledge in this area. If you currently have a trust, or are thinking of setting up one, this book will show you some common mistakes and how to avoid them. If you are currently a trustee or future trustee, you will realize that becoming a trustee means accepting a lot of responsibilities. There are many decisions that need to be made over the life of a trust, many of which are not pleasant to make. Some have absolutely nothing to do with assets or money—yet they must be faced. The more aware you are of the potential problems, the better trustee you will become.

I started doing research to see what else I could learn to benefit the trustees of my clients. Sadly, there was a lack of information out there for the actual trustee, because advisors cannot make money from the trustee once the trust has already been set up. No one wants to tackle the information. The lack of information led me to write this book. Such information is becoming more necessary over time, due to the overall average increase in age. It is important that a trustee realizes his or her responsibility to the trust and the potential mistakes and pitfalls that may arise.

Most of the advice I provide, I learned the hard way. I was almost the victim of a lawsuit brought on by one of the heirs of my client. The case was truly an experience, and even though it was difficult at the time, I learned more from this incident than any school or book could have prepared me for.

The case portrays almost every mistake you can make as a trustee. Some mistakes were avoided, some were not. The case shows that to be a good trustee, you need to do a lot more work than just managing the assets inside the trust. I developed a seminar based on this family to illustrate the most common mistakes, but I found that I could not share all the details in such a short time.

The same case in the seminar is discussed in this book in more detail. The details are essential to fully understand how to avoid these mistakes. I changed the names to protect the individuals that took part, but be assured that all of the events are real. I worked with this family for years. They were an average family just like yours and mine. They shared the same hopes, desires, and problems of almost every middle-class family in our country. The couple who left the trust was not super-wealthy. The husband was a blue-collar worker and the wife was a homemaker. They saved their money well over the years and amassed comfortable savings to retire on. The couple was just unfortunate enough to have greedy children.

The case of Norman and Margaret Sample is the most eye-opening case of my past ten years. It was not a very complicated estate to set up. Even after the set up, they followed my advice. All the heirs were to divide everything up evenly, and the government was not going to get any of it. Everything should have been smooth. It was in an indisputable trust, until the relatives came into the picture. The case of the Samples changed my outlook on an important responsibility—the importance of a trustee's role once taking control of the assets.

The Story of the Samples

Norman Sample lived through the Great Depression and, as a result, developed the "Depression-era mentality" when it came to money. He was very frugal in everything he did. He would use something until it was worn out before considering replacing it. Then he would search for the best bargain available to replace whatever it was. When it came to saving money, Norman kept his hands on every penny. In fact, he was the type of person who would pick up change on the streets, even if it was a penny, and save it. He certainly had no problem with the concept of saving for a rainy day. As far as investing money went, the largest risk he would take was a certificate of deposit. Norman was far more concerned with keeping the money he had saved, rather than invest in some riskier investments with a higher potential income.

Norman was a blue-collar worker who paid his union dues and retired with full benefits when the time came. He was not a wealthy man, but he built up sizable savings through this thriftiness and steady retirement income. He was not afraid of hard work and always kept busy, even in retirement. His passion was to travel. He had a recreational vehicle and was not afraid to put miles on it. He loved the open countryside and was always planning to visit new places. His frequent traveling led him and his wife, Margaret, to Wyoming on one occasion. They found a spot they absolutely adored and bought a vacation house so they would have a place to travel and get away.

Margaret shared Norman's outlook when it came to finances. Margaret came from a very poor background. She did not like showy, gaudy things. She liked to save money as well and knew the value of a dollar. Margaret worked as a volunteer for the Red Cross. She was grossly overweight a few years before she met Norman. She went on a diet after the doctor told her that she was in poor health and might not live much longer. Over a six-month period, she lost about 120 pounds. She was in much better health. Margaret had a better outlook on life and enjoyed traveling with Norman.

Both Norman and Margaret had been married before meeting one another. Norman's first wife, Betsy, had died a few years earlier. She did not suffer long, but did spend some time in a nursing home. Norman loved her, and it really hurt to lose her. At that time, he felt that he would never find another person to share his life with. He watched Betsy slowly lose her dignity at the nursing home and swore it would never happen to him. Betsy and Norman had only one daughter, whom they tragically outlived. From this one daughter, Norman had a grandson. The grandson was the only surviving relative Norman had.

Margaret was married to a man whom she also loved dearly. He was killed suddenly in an automobile accident several years prior to meeting Norman. She raised three children on her own after she lost her husband. She, too, felt that she would never find another person to take his place. She was passing time, keeping busy, but not very happy.

Norman and Margaret met at church. It was innocent at first. Norman just enjoyed Margaret's company. They became good friends, and eventually fell in love. They were married shortly afterward and did not look back. Both of them could not believe their good fortune in finding someone they could love so much so late in life. They were very much the newlyweds. They just had a good time together, laughing all the time. They were both very excited about their marriage. Norman, for example, was retired and wanted to enjoy life with the woman he loved. He had friends throughout the country, so he wanted Margaret to travel with him to meet them all. They tried to enjoy every minute together.

Norman lived in a house in Bonita, California, for over thirty years. Behind his house there was a smaller guesthouse. For the last ten years the same lady, Elsie, lived there. Norman only charged her $200 per month for rent. He told me that as long as he was alive, she would have a place to live. She was a kind, older lady, several years older than Norman. But even though she was older, she was very healthy. She maintained the garden and took care of the property for Norman. In fact, Elsie woke up at the crack of dawn every morning to work on her flower beds. She planted all sorts of fruit trees and vegetables in Norman's yard. Elsie took good care of the yard, and it looked absolutely beautiful. Elsie even took care of the house when Norman and

Margaret traveled, which was quite often. It kept her very busy, but it was more of a hobby than a chore. Elsie was afraid of living alone, so she loved staying at Norman's guest house. Living in the guest house allowed her to be independent without the loneliness. Norman did not mind, because he enjoyed Elsie's company. When Norman and Margaret were married, Elsie and Margaret became very close friends. Margaret was not a big gardener, but she would go out and keep Elsie company while she took care of her flowers. Margaret realized that even though it was technically her yard, it belonged to Elsie. It was all Elsie had left.

I first met Norman and Margaret at one of my seminars on estate planning. They were sitting together closely in the back of the room, listening with great intensity. Their bodies were leaned forward and their eyes were filled with curiosity. I could tell they were going to be an extraordinary client, because several times during the presentation I noticed Norman nudging Margaret and then briefly whisper something in her ear. They seemed to relate with most of the ideas that I was presenting in the seminar. As the seminar went on, Norman began actively participating in the discussions. Margaret, on the other hand, just sat listening to every word. Margaret did not say much that day, but I could tell she was taking this information very seriously. After the presentation, they came up to me and introduced themselves. The Samples had very warm handshakes. They told me they were impressed by the presentation and wanted to set up a meeting with me to discuss their situation.

When I met Norman and Margaret at their house the following week, I could tell right away they were a unique couple. They were always showing their affection towards each other through secret glances and occasional touches. I was somewhat surprised to find out they had only been married for a little over a year. They behaved as if they had spent a lifetime together. They seemed to think as one. For instance, Norman would start a sentence and Margaret would finish it.

Norman and Margaret came to me for financial advice on their future together. They had both experienced enormous losses already in their lives. They both knew that eventually one of them would be alone again. They wanted solid plans this time around; everything must be planned and taken care of in advance.

Norman, in particular, was concerned about staying in a nursing home. He saw Betsy go through it and did not want to share her experience. He also felt the financial drain of a long-term stay in a nursing home. As their financial planner, my first task insured that if he or Margaret should need long-term care, it would not impact their lifestyle. During one of my meetings with the Samples, Norman confided in me that he never wanted to end up in a nursing home and would avoid it at all costs. I still remember what he told me. Norman put his hand on my shoulder and said, "Sandeep, I want you to know something. We are buying this policy because you're recommending it, and we trust you. However, I want to make it clear to you that if you think that I'm ever going to use this policy, I'd much rather use my .44 first." I remember it so clearly because I really did not know what to say to him at the time—I didn't know how to react.

The Samples were also concerned about Norman's grandson, Greg. Greg was Norman's only surviving relative. For the last two years, Greg worked as a claims adjuster. He was 42 years old and had lived in San Diego his whole life. Greg's mother died when he was young, and he was raised by his father, Jim. Greg was not well educated and was always looking for a quick way to get rich. Unfortunately, he never got much money that way. Greg lost a lot of his savings investing in commodities. He did not share his grandfather's financial mentality and struggled financially.

Luckily, Greg's wife, Sue, made a decent living as a waitress. In the past, she was involved with different kinds of multi-level marketing. She worked very hard at everything she did. Sue grew up in a poor, dysfunctional family, and became a dominant, controlling person, especially in her marriage. Norman noticed this and it concerned him.

Norman told me that Greg was not happy with his marriage to Margaret. Greg thought Margaret only married him for his money, even though that was clearly not the case. Greg was concerned about his inheritance and was not very friendly towards Margaret. Greg was the only relative that did not come to their wedding and refused to come to the birthday parties at the Samples' house.

The Samples were concerned that if something happened to Norman before Margaret, Greg would attempt to take away Margaret's current lifestyle. Her biggest fear was that Greg would evict her from their house. She did not want to be in a position where she had to look for a home at such a late stage in her life. Margaret was terrified of Greg and did not know how to act, because Greg expressed such animosity towards her.

One day after Norman and Margaret returned home from Wyoming, they realized that a few items were moved around and some missing. Apparently, Greg used his key to get inside their house and went through all of their belongings. Norman and Margaret felt violated that Greg would do such a thing. After all, this was their grandson and they trusted him. Greg's lack of respect added to the Samples' concern for their future.

Over the next few months, I met with the Samples several times. Each time, we discussed their concerns and goals. They wanted a smooth plan for the rest of their lives. It was going to be a challenge, but certainly not the most difficult case I ever tackled. Eventually, I was responsible for their entire financial future and had a trust set up for them. The living trust eliminated Margaret's concerns about future housing. It ensured she would have a place to live for the rest of her life. They had long-term insurance to protect their estate from any long-term disability they might develop in the future. I also managed their investments. I gradually began to take over small parts of the investments. We all felt it was best to move slowly, based on both Norman and Margaret's strong aversion to risk. Their attitude towards their investments and risk changed over time through the relationship we developed. I was able to give them a much better rate of return through fixed annuities and very conservative stocks and bonds. I did everything I could to take the burden of planning off of them. They were very happy and relieved to have someone they trusted to turn to for advice. I was very confident in our plan and did not even consider the amount of problems that would show up later.

Most of the planning was complete, with the exception of one major detail. Norman and Margaret needed a trustee. While they were still alive, Norman and Margaret would be the trustees. They could successfully manage their own trust, because they knew their own goals and would work towards them. But if they were mentally unable to attend to their own needs, then someone would need to take over for them. Norman and Margaret wanted to choose a trustee to manage their trust in case they became unable to do it themselves.

The majority of the money in the estate originally belonged to Norman. Although Margaret's input weighed heavily, it was Norman's ultimate right to decide on the trustee. The problem was Norman had limited options on his side of the family. Norman's only daughter and sister died several years earlier. His sister, Harriet, left Norman her estate because he was her only living relative. Since Greg was Norman's only relative left, he wanted to make him the trustee. But Greg did not prove to be trustworthy or financially mature.

Norman had another dilemma because Margaret was afraid of what Greg would do to her. As a husband, Norman wanted to make sure his wife was well taken care of after he was gone. If Greg was the trustee, it would defeat the purpose of setting up the trust to protect Margaret. Norman wanted to trust Greg so, being his grandfather, Norman wanted to give Greg the benefit of the doubt.

Norman and Margaret decided to test Greg's financial maturity. They felt they might have misjudged him and wanted to give him every opportunity to prove himself. They invited Greg over for dinner without telling him anything. Greg did not realize this, but this evening would change his life in many ways.

Norman and Margaret were very anxious about their dinner with Greg. Margaret spent all day in the kitchen preparing her famous roast beef and Greg's favorite apple pie. She even cleaned the house so that it was spotless. When Greg finally arrived, he did not notice all the trouble the Samples had gone through. During dinner he was very quiet. He did not thank or appreciate the good silverware they used or the dinner Margaret cooked. But Norman tried to ignore all that. After dinner, Norman sat down with Greg in the living room. He told him how much he loved and cared for him as a grandson. Norman explained to Greg that he wanted to show him his true feelings by sharing Harriet's inheritance with him. Greg knew that Norman had received an inheritance from his Aunt Harriet, although he did not know exactly how much the inheritance was worth. Greg did not get anything from the inheritance, so

Norman wanted to give him something. After a long pause, Norman went into the study and wrote Greg a check for $100,000. He told Greg he could do with it as he pleased, but gave him my name and telephone number with the hope he would invest it wisely. Norman watched Greg's every move. Greg took a quick glance at the check and put it in his back pocket. Greg did not properly thank Norman for the gift. He acted as if Norman's money already belonged to him. Norman wanted so badly to trust Greg with his money that he turned the other way and ignored Greg's reaction.

Meanwhile, I was unaware of this test. I might have recommended something a little more tax friendly, but I could see their reasoning. Norman called me several weeks afterward and asked if I had heard from his grandson. He explained the whole test to me. Regrettably, I had not heard a word. Within six months Norman discovered that Greg had spent his entire gift. He bought a new truck and lots of clothes. He and Sue also took several vacations and lived it up. Greg did not see this money as a gift, but rather as a down payment of the money he thought he was going to receive from the inheritance.

Norman was furious, but it also made his decision about Greg as a possible trustee very easy. He knew that Greg could not be trusted. Furthermore, Norman could not put his wife in a position where she was uncomfortable. Norman contemplated about what he wanted to do with his money. Should he just spend it all or not doing anything at all? At this point, Norman was so angry at Greg that he didn't care if Greg never got a dime of his money. Norman was left in a situation where he had to consider his only relative unfit for this responsibility. He knew it was better to keep the money in the family, even if it was not blood-related family. Based on his decision, Norman wanted to explore other candidates for the trustee on Margaret's side of the family.

Margaret had three children from her previous marriage. The oldest daughter, Marsha, was in her early fifties. She was divorced three times and was in her fourth marriage. She was a realtor and was struggling with her career. Her husband, Sam, was not working and had no a job for a long time. They lived in St. Louis and did not communicate with Norman and Margaret very often, except during the holidays. Sam and Marsha had a very poor financial record. They did not have any savings and lived month to month with bills controlling their lives.

While I was managing the Samples' finances, Sam and Marsha came to San Diego. Sam approached Norman with a business idea, needing financing assistance from him. Sam had a small business plan, so Norman brought it over to my office to have it evaluated. After looking it over, I found several things that raised caution flags in my mind. He wanted about $200,000, with 80% of the investment going to his salary and other intangible items. Norman and Margaret were well off, but I did not feel they could afford to just write off the money. If something bad happened and the creditors come calling, they would be the last to see any money. Based on this, I recommended against the investment. Norman told me he felt the same way but was looking for a second opinion. He ended up giving Sam around $5000 to help him out. Norman felt he could rule out Marsha, based on her inability to manage money, her distance from them, and the fact that he felt Sam and Marsha already had their eyes on his money.

Margaret's youngest son, Peter, was not a possible trustee either. He only lived three miles away and rarely visited. He cared more about drinking than anything else. He was in his late thirties, had never been married, and did not work regularly. He was more involved in his own life than the lives of his relatives.

The more Norman thought about it, the more he realized there were several people banking on a large inheritance. He was not vindictive—he cared for them and wanted them all to get a share of his life's savings, despite their shortcomings.

The last option was Margaret's middle daughter, Janet. Fortunately, she was a very responsible woman. She was in her mid-forties, married to the same man for twenty years, had kids still in school and was an elementary school teacher. She enjoyed clipping coupons during her spare time because she was thrifty at heart. Janet lived close to San Diego and visited Norman and Margaret often. She and Norman got along great from the beginning. She took an active role in the planning of Norman and Margaret's wedding and made herself available for them if they needed her. Norman and Margaret felt they could always count on her.

It was not a tough decision to pick a trustee, but they wanted to be fair so they looked at each individual, listing the strengths and weaknesses of each. After evaluating everyone, Norman and Margaret made the decision to have Janet become their trustee. This was one of the most important decisions Norman and Margaret would make in their lives together. They did it correctly by not rushing into anything or committing to anyone in a hurry. In my opinion, Janet made an excellent trustee. She was very honest and cared about her parents. After Norman and Margaret decided to make Janet the trustee, they had to decide whether or not they should actually tell her about it. They also discussed whether or not they should tell her the financial details of the estate and if so, how much? After many discussions, the Samples decided they were comfortable with Janet knowing the details of the estate. They thought it would be best to tell her everything.

Norman and Margaret wanted to tell Janet their decision over dinner at their house. Once again, Margaret spent all day cooking and cleaning the house. Janet arrived at the Samples' home just as Margaret was bringing out the bread from the oven. The warm smell of fresh bread quickly filled the home. Janet had no idea why they had called her there that evening, but knew there must be something special. I met Janet for the very first time at this dinner. I was invited to the dinner to explain all the technical details and answer any questions Janet might have. Her confidence and ease at accepting me at this family meeting impressed me.

Dinner was absolutely magnificent. We talked about grand-children, politics, and the recent trip the Samples went on. Norman even cracked a couple jokes. There was never a quiet moment. Finally, Norman looked at his watch and announced that it was time to discuss something more serious. Janet looked at Norman with curiosity. The mood in the room quickly changed. Norman began by saying that lately he and Margaret had been thinking a lot about their future and the futures of their children and grandchildren. They had both lost their first spouses, so they knew that proper planning was important. They realized that they were not getting any younger and must face the fact that eventually they would both be gone.

I watched Janet throughout the entire time. She seemed to be growing more and more uncomfortable by the minute. Finally, Norman announced they had made some major decisions recently. He went to the study and pulled out a leather-bound notebook called a trust from the bookshelf. Norman came back to the dining room and placed the trust on the table. As he was opening the book to the first page, Norman told Janet that they had set up all their estate into a trust to prepare to pass it on to their heirs. Most importantly, they wanted Janet to be the trustee of that trust when the time came they could no longer control it effectively.

But before Norman could finish the conversation, Janet got up from her chair and started pacing back and forth with her hand on her forehead. She was obviously surprised at what Norman just told her. She replied, "Mom, Dad! Stop and listen to me. I can't believe you two are talking about this kind of stuff! It's not an important subject right now. The two of you have many years left. You both are healthy and hardly ever sick. Besides, I don't even want to think about losing the two of you."

She continued to argue that it was not right for a daughter to know so much about her parents' financial affairs. Besides, it was their money. They should spend their hard-earned money on themselves and take a trip to see the world. They should not worry about the children. All the children were doing just fine. This subject should not be discussed until the time was right. Janet said all this with full conviction, but I later found out that in the back of her mind she was asking, "What's a trustee?" She had no clue, but she knew she did not want to talk about it because she did not want to think about her mother and step-father dying.

As a financial advisor, I tried to convince Janet that this decision was important and should be discussed—it just seemed easier for everyone to ignore the problem. Janet apologized for having me come out all this way for nothing, but she just did not feel it necessary at this time. Norman offered a mild protest, but he could see she was adamant. He did not know how to react. He picked up the trust, went back to the study, and put the trust back in its original space on the shelf. The trust sat on the shelf to collect dust for a couple years.

After that night, Norman and Margaret planned a big trip to visit their good friends Phil and Bernice in Seattle. With all the chaos going on at home, Norman and Margaret were look-ing forward to their annual trip to Seattle. During this time of year, Phil and Norman loved to go fishing. Every year they engaged in a little friendly competition to see who could catch the biggest fish. Last year Norman won and he was determined to keep his title.

But just a couple weeks before the trip, Norman suddenly had a stroke and was rushed to the hospital. It turned out to be a mild stroke, but it affected the left side of his body. He was a very stubborn man and refused to acknowledge it or let it slow him down. Up to this point, he was rarely ill. He was used to working through an illness. In his mind, he decided he would just work through this one as well. But over a week's time, Norman unexpectedly lost movement in his leg and relied on a walker.

Margaret was worried and insisted they postpone the trip, but Norman was determined. The only thing Margaret could do was convince Norman to go to the doctor. The doctor, of course, highly recommended the Samples' stay in town so he could run more tests on Norman. Norman realized his condition was much more serious than he thought, so he reluctantly agreed to stay.

After the stroke, life for the Samples became difficult. Norman had trouble walking and relied on his walker more each day. In addition, his speech was becoming slurred. Norman was frustrated at his condition. He felt out of control and helpless. Margaret tried to help Norman as much as possible, but there was not much she could do. Norman was stubborn and refused to let people help him.

Margaret called me about six months after the stroke. She complained of a headache and sounded very tired and stressed.

She had a very high-pitched voice, almost gasping for air. She wanted to make sure all their finances were in order, the estate was all in the trust, all the papers signed, and that there was nothing left for them to do. I assured her that, as I had told her several times in the past year, everything was in order. She told me about Norman and how worried she was for him. She was scared. All I could do was tell her she had nothing to worry about financially. I told her I could come out to their house the next week. This would be an easy way to calm her fears. The Samples were such kind people that I always enjoyed visiting them. They always gave me fresh baked cookies to bring home. It was something little, but I knew my service meant a lot to them. Margaret felt better and told me that it would be nice to see me again. So before Margaret and I hung up, we set up an appointment for the following week.

The very next day I received a phone call. At first, I didn't recognize the voice on the other end because it sounded like a child. I could hear breathing over the phone. The person sounded so hurt. I heard a sniffle; it was Norman. "She's dead, Sandeep, she's dead.... It happened last night..... she was.... sleeping." It was the first time I heard Norman cry. The cry was so painful. It sounded as if a piece of him died along with Margaret. I felt so bad for Norman and tried to comfort him. But I could not believe the news. I was shocked.

Norman wanted to be the one to call me. He told me the details and that he was glad she went peacefully. He wanted to meet with me as soon as possible to discuss what he needed to do. I told him of the meeting Margaret and I had set up the following week. We agreed to meet the day after her funeral. I thought it a bit strange that Norman would be concerned with his finances so soon after Margaret's death. Norman was always a practical man who dealt with problems head-on. I assumed he was getting pressure from her children to deal with it this way. My suspicions were confirmed the following week.

My wife, Nisha, and I attended Margaret's funeral. There was a viewing of Margaret's body, followed by a service. At the viewing, my wife and I kept to ourselves to let the family grieve in private. I spoke briefly to Norman when I first arrived and expressed my sympathy. I also noticed Janet and expressed my sorrow to her. She had done a beautiful job planning the funeral for her mother.

Greg and Margaret's son, Peter, soon approached me. They introduced themselves to me and said they needed to talk to me in private. I mentioned that since this was a sensitive time, they should call and make an appointment with my office. They insisted it would not take long and wanted to talk now. Seeing there was little I could do that would not draw attention, I reluctantly agreed. They said that since Margaret was now gone, Norman needed assistance with his investments. They felt that mentally he was not capable of such important decisions. They felt they should now be making the decisions and my services would no longer be needed. I was somewhat taken aback, not because I was being shut out of Norman's financial affairs but by all their anxious greed at Margaret's funeral. She had not even been buried yet!

As politely as possible, I told them Norman was in charge of his own finances. If he decided they should handle his affairs, then it was fine with me, but he had to make that decision. Peter and Greg did not know Janet was set up to be the Samples' trustee. Of course, I was not going to bring up this subject. If they wanted to make an issue out of this, it would have to be done at my office, not at Margaret's funeral.

I should have realized then there was going to be trouble. This incident shows a lot about Peter and Greg's character. They were motivated by money, not genuine concern. It is easy now to look back and pick out all the events that indicated I was going to have problems with the family members. It is difficult to believe that blood relatives could value money more than their relationships.

When I met with Norman later that week, I did not mention my talk with Greg and Peter. Instead, I explained to him everything we had already set up in the trust in detail. Norman kept asking me that if something happened to him, what would happen to his estate? He was concerned if he could no longer handle his finances, then who would take over? I explained again and again, through various scenarios, that Janet would be in charge. He finally seemed satisfied. He then revealed to me that Greg and Peter had come to him, wanting to take control of the family finances. He explained to them he was still in charge, but did not tell them that Janet was the trustee if anything should happen to him. Then I told Norman of my brief discussion with them at Margaret's funeral. Norman became very angry. He realized what they were tying to do. But he sat back and just smiled. He knew there was little they could do to take over and was confident in the trust we had set up. Norman did not want to exclude them from the estate, but he also did not want them controlling it.

At this meeting, I realized that Norman was in poor health. His memory was slipping and his ability to comprehend difficult concepts was not what it used to be. It was the result of the stroke he had suffered earlier. I called Janet to express my concerns to keep an eye on Norman. She agreed his health was failing and was worried about what would happen when the rest of the family discovered this. I warned her they already knew about it.

The following week, I received a phone call from a lawyer who I knew professionally. The lawyer told me that she was retained by Greg about handling the Samples' estate. She wanted to talk to me to find out more about the finances of the estate. I was a little surprised, but I told her there was a trust in place and a trustee named. I mentioned that the trustee was not Greg, so the information of the estate could not be discussed without permission from Norman. The lawyer was unaware of the Samples' trust. She told me that if she had known about it, she would have told Greg there was no case from the beginning. The trust was indisputable.

Later that same day, I received another phone call from another lawyer. This lawyer was representing Peter. It was basically the same story. The lawyer wanted to know more information about the Samples' estate. I told this lawyer the same thing I had told the previous one; I was not allowed to discuss the financial details because a trust was already set up. When I explained to him about the trust and the fact that Peter was not named the trustee, he quickly dropped the case.

Believe it or not, I received a third call that same day from another lawyer. This lawyer was representing Greg's father, Henry. He did not want to be left out either. Jim was looking out for Greg's best interest and wanted to do everything he could for his son. Again, I explained to the lawyer the whole situation. Once he heard that Greg was not the trustee, he dropped the case.

I still do not know if the three of them were working together or individually, but they were aware of their situation. They knew about the trust, but did not know who the trustee was. There were not too many choices left, though. As I told them at Margaret's funeral, I was not allowed legally to discuss Norman's situation with them without Norman's permission. I was certain Norman was not going to give them permission either.

I thought this would be the end of the lawyers, but two weeks later a different lawyer called me regarding the same thing. The lawyer was very aggressive and wanted to know the financial details of the Samples' estate. But when I told him about the trust, he claimed he had not known anything about it and promptly ended the call.

That was the last I heard from the lawyers. It seems that proper planning does pay off in certain circumstances. I thought this would be the end of Greg and Peter. In fact, it was only the beginning. They just laid low for awhile.

I told Norman about all the lawyers that had called me. He was very irritated about the news. Greg and Peter picked a bad time to upset Norman. Norman didn't even want to deal with them. Norman was very depressed with the lost of his wife. Margaret was everything to him. He took her death very hard. He had lost two wives in less than six years. After Betsy's death, he had been depressed, but eventually moved on with life. Now, as a result of the stroke, he did not have the same energy and drive he once had. The stroke affected his mobility and depression affected his mental ability. Overall, Norman was in bad shape.

I was so concerned about Norman's condition that I set up a meeting with Janet, Norman and his attorney. Norman's condition was deteriorating quickly. He was having trouble getting around without his walker and was gaining lots of weight because he was not as active as he used to be. He was no longer participating in the community and spent most of his time watching TV. Norman's sluggish lifestyle added to his depression. At our meeting, we all expressed our concern to Norman. We suggested it was best for Norman to resign as the trustee of the trust and let Janet take over. Norman took a long, deep breath. As he was letting it out, he looked at Janet and nodded his head. He trusted Janet and knew she could handle the job. Norman resigned as the trustee of the estate.

When Janet took over the trust, the family was surprised. This was the first time they heard of Janet in this position. They all assumed that Greg would be Norman's trustee. I could tell from Greg's body language that he was furious and offended about Janet's new position. After all, he expected to become the trustee and was humiliated in front of the family. But, somehow, Greg managed to keep his cool when the announcement was made.

As trustee, Janet decided to do what as safe, simple and convenient with Norman's investments. She moved his assets into CDs and fixed annuities at her local bank. She fired me thinking she wouldn't need any professional advice for the trust. Janet also decided that Elsie could no longer handle Norman by herself. Elsie was getting older, and simple tasks were becoming more difficult for her. It was not fair to expect Elsie to take on Norman's burdens.

A few incidents happened that made Janet realize Elsie needed more help with Norman. For instance, once Norman backed out of the garage before opening the door. Janet also found out that Norman accidentally set his pants on fire while ironing. After these incidents, Janet knew she had to hire some-one full-time. Norman did not require special attention; he was lonely and just needed someone to watch him. She happened to know of a family member who was currently looking for a job. Janet knew that her relative, Chris, would do a good job because

Norman and Chris had a lot in common. For instance, they were both huge Padres fans and enjoyed watching sports. Chris did not have any formal training in the care of elders, but he was perfect for the job and could be trusted. When Norman first met Chris, Janet knew she had made the right decision. They became immediate friends and enjoyed each other's company very much.

Because of Norman's Depression-era mentality, Norman dealt with all transactions on a cash basis. He viewed banks as a necessary evil. Norman did not believe in buying on credit, or even writing checks. When Margaret was alive, she balanced the checkbook, so Norman did not keep detailed records of his account. He only cared if he had money or not. When he ran out of cash, he asked Janet to withdraw money from the bank for his needs. Norman worried about having enough cash on hand to do what he wanted, so Janet agreed to bring him cash every time she came to visit. Janet ended up withdrawing cash for Norman several times a week.

Norman spent most of his money eating out. When Margaret was still alive, she did all the cooking. Occasionally, they went out to eat at their favorite restaurant, Jackey's. Jackey's was a family-run restaurant near the Samples' home. As time went on, Norman and Margaret became regulars and ate there daily for breakfast, lunch and dinner. Every time they had the special of the day. The owners loved the Samples and treated them specially.

Now that Margaret was gone, Norman ate every meal at Jackey's because he did not cook. Janet found out about Norman's situation and arranged for the restaurant to deliver to the house on the days Norman could not make it in. She used this arrangement to keep track of how Norman was doing, because he was not always honest about how he felt. Janet also found out that Chris covered for Norman. Chris liked Norman and didn't want Norman to look like he could not get around by himself. So Janet was able to keep tabs on Norman by his visits to Jackey's. Norman was eventually eating every meal in his house. He had difficulty walking and was confined to his house. Janet became worried and confronted Chris about it. He admitted that Norman needed more help and special attention with simple daily tasks, like using the restroom and bathing, that he could not give him.

Janet sat down with Norman to talk about his worsening condition. Norman's eyes reminded Janet of a young child, who was lost and helpless. She told Norman that she was concerned he needed help that neither she nor Chris could provide. Janet took a deep breath and held Norman's hand between hers. She gave Norman's hand a light squeeze and told him it would be best to check him into a nursing home where he would receive all the attention he needed. Norman stared at Janet for a moment. He could tell she was worrying too much about him. He looked at Janet and reluctantly nodded. Norman appeared to have a different attitude about long-term care facilities now. It was less than a year since Margaret's death and Norman seemed to have lost the will to live. Norman's memory was also fading. One minute he would be having a conversation with Janet, and the next minute he would be in another conversation twenty years ago. Norman realized his condition was getting much worse and that he did need special attention. Norman agreed with Janet about checking him into a facility near her house where she could visit often.

Janet visited Norman all the time and kept him company when no one else would. The other relatives did not spend much time visiting Norman. They were very busy in their lives and did not stop by to see how Norman was doing. Luckily for Norman, Janet kept a constant watch on him. She came by several times a week because Norman was having difficulty getting adjusted to the nursing home. Norman didn't like giving up his old lifestyle, so Janet continued to bring him things every time she came to visit, such as meals from Jackey's to help him feel at home. She was very busy with her own life, as well as taking care of Norman. She did this because she felt responsible as a trustee, but mostly because she genuinely cared for the man who became her second father so late in life.

When Greg found out that Norman was in a nursing home, he was suspicious of Janet's actions. Greg was still upset about the trusteeship and did not communicate at all with Janet. In fact, he never even went in to visit Norman in the nursing home. He felt like he was in the dark about his grandfather and wanted to know what was going on. Greg was convinced Janet was putting Norman in a nursing home against his will. After all, he knew his grandfather's fear of a long-term care facility. In order to get information about what was going on, Greg persuaded Elsie that Norman was being put in a nursing home against his wishes and that Janet was abusing her position as a trustee. He asked her assistance in getting more information about Norman. Together they stole Norman's mail and managed to get copies of Norman's financial statements. They realized how much Norman was worth from these documents.

Greg visited Norman twice after discovering how much he was worth. Unfortunately, the visits resulted in Norman being in bad shape after Greg visited. The first time Greg came to visit, he marched into the nursing home and handed Norman documents that gave Greg full power to Norman's estate. Norman was very irritated and angry, even though he never signed any papers. Greg's visits did not help Norman's high blood pressure; in fact, Norman's overall health got much worse after the visits. He was often so upset about Greg that the nurses had to bring him sedatives to calm him down. Because of this, the nursing home denied Greg access to Norman without supervision or permission from Janet. Even in Norman's weakened mental state, he was aware of Greg's greed.

When Greg could not get Norman to sign over the trusteeship, he tried another tactic. He approached the administration at the nursing home and claimed Norman was being held there against his will. The administrators knew the situation well. They knew that Norman was in no condition to take care of himself. They listened to Greg, but calmly explained to him that it was in Norman's best interests if he stayed at the nursing home. Greg took this all in stride. He was not about to let this get in the way of Norman's money. Greg went to the local authorities and complained that the nursing home was mistreating his grandfather. The local authorities investigated the nursing home and Janet in-depth. Greg thought they were both conspiring against him. They found that not only was Norman not being mistreated but was in need of constant, round-the-clock care. These were not Greg's desired results.

Since he got no satisfaction from this investigation, he contacted the state authorities. He claimed the local authorities were corrupt and not capable of handling the investigation. He caused another investigation at the state level. This involved investigating everyone previously involved, in addition to the local authorities. All of this put a tremendous strain of time, energy and frustration on Janet because she constantly had to prove herself in front of people who did not know the situation. On top of that, Janet was juggling her career as a schoolteacher, wife, mother, and her care for Norman. They were listening to Greg's lies and had to act on them. Of course, all this resulted in absolutely nothing, except for wasted time and taxpayers money. There was no corruption at the local level and Norman really did need help. They also found that Janet was doing everything she could to provide for Norman.

As if Janet did not have enough to worry about with the investigations and Norman's health, one morning she received a phone call from one of Norman's old neighbors. Apparently,

Elsie had accidentally left the water on when she was working on the garden. She had left it on all night and the ground had become soft and weak. It caused a major landslide and a section of Norman's yard ended up on the neighbor's house down below. It did extensive damage, approximately $25,000 worth. As the trustee, it was Janet's responsibility. The insurance company investigated and determined the cause of the damage was neglect. They told Janet they would pay the bill because Norman had been a customer for over twenty-five years. But if something like this happened again, they would not cover it. Janet realized that being a trustee was much more complicated than she ever thought. She knew she had to reduce the liability on the estate. It was obvious Elsie was no longer able to take care of things herself. One of the toughest decisions Janet ever had to make was when she decided that Elsie could no longer live there. She had to evict Elsie, even though it was against Norman's wishes. Her job, first and foremost, was to protect the estate, and she intended to do that.

When Janet first put Norman in the nursing home, she was not sure how much it would cost. At that time, she was only concerned about the reputation of the facility rather than the cost. She was quite astonished to find out that Norman's nursing home was $3800 a month. She was so shocked that she immediately called me as soon as she found out. Up to this point, Janet didn't really think about long-term care issues. To her surprise, I informed her that Norman and Margaret set up a long-term care policy several years ago. Even though Margaret never used a dime, Norman's policy paid for 100% of the total cost. I smiled at Janet as she let out a huge sigh of relief.

After two years in a nursing home, Norman's health took a turn for the worse. He came down with a severe case of pneumonia. His condition got so bad that the nursing home transported him into a hospital. When Janet was visiting Norman in the hospital, the doctor took her aside to discuss Norman's health. The doctor explained to Janet there were decisions that needed to be made for Norman. Norman was very uncomfortable and his condition was getting much worse. The doctor said they could try an expensive operation that did not have a high probability of survival or they could just let nature take its course. The doctor advised Janet against the operation because there were too many risks involved with Norman's old age and a chance that Norman might not recover from the operation. Janet thought this decision through thoroughly. But it was not very difficult. She wanted to try anything that might help Norman. She went against the doctor's recommendation and Norman went through the operation. Luckily, the operation turned out to be a success. Norman fully recovered, but six months later he developed another unrelated case of pneumonia.

One day when Janet was in the middle of class, she received an emergency phone call from the nursing home. The nursing home rushed Norman to the hospital because his condition once again took a change for the worse. There was nothing that could be done. They just wanted Norman to be comfortable. When Janet heard about this, she left class early and rushed to the hospital to be with Norman. She knew the end was near. Throughout the day, Janet held Norman's hand and gave him words of encouragement. Occasionally, Norman would glance over at Janet and take a deep breath of air as if he was trying to say something. Norman was in a lot of pain trying to breathe. Even he knew his end was near.

Janet stayed with Norman all night until he finally feel asleep. As she was leaving, she took one last glance at Norman and slowly closed the door. She knew the end would one day come, but she didn't want it to happen now. But the next morning, Norman passed away. He died in his sleep very peacefully. Janet was upset but knew he was not very happy the past few years. She knew that Norman was now in a better place with Margaret.

Norman's funeral took place several days later. Beautiful flowers surrounded Norman's final resting place. Norman was buried next to Margaret as a symbol of eternal love. Greg was upset by this because he wanted Norman to be buried next to Norman's first wife, Betsy; but there was nothing he could do, because Norman was the one who had made the decision. Primarily, family members attended Norman's funeral. Everyone was dressed in dark Sunday clothes. To my surprise, less than a dozen people total attended the whole event. I remember thinking how ironic the white chairs looked with everyone's dark attire. With just a handful of people, there was just a sea of white, empty chairs. It was sad. Norman lived a long life and had many friends throughout his life, but not many people showed up. It made me think about all the relationships he must have developed along the way and all the experiences he went through. I realized Norman was unhappy the last few years of his life because he was unable to do the things he really loved, such as traveling and visiting his friends. It was because Norman was confined to the nursing home that he lost touch with the rest of the world.

After the funeral, Janet called to inform me that everything with the funeral was already taken care of. She wanted to know what the next step was. I told her that we needed to set up a time with their attorney and the family members to go over the final reading and distribution of the trust. We decided to do this as soon as possible and agreed to meet everyone the following week at the attorney's office. Before I got off the phone with Janet, she made it a point to tell me that Greg had sent beautiful flowers to Norman's funeral; but later that same day, she received the bill for those flowers. I couldn't help laughing. It was an amusing story of the events that were about to happen.

Before the distribution of the inheritance, the estate taxes (death taxes) had to be paid off by the family members. At the time of Norman's death, the estate was worth over 1.5 million dollars. Because estate taxes are collected after the death of the last spouse, the family had to pay $94,768.12 in taxes. This amount of money did not go well with the family, especially Greg. They were all amazed at the extraordinary output. But they realized there was really no way around it. They finally all agreed to pay the taxes so that they could get their inheritance as soon as possible.

The following week, Janet, Marsha, Peter, Greg and I met at the law firm for the final reading of the will. I could feel the tension building as we sat around the large marble conference table, waiting for the attorney to arrive. The room was quiet except for the occasional rustling of papers. It was as if everyone was lost in their own world of thoughts. It was amazing how silence could be so awkward.

When the attorney arrived, he gave a copy of the trust to everyone in the family. We began with the distribution of the trust. The first distribution went to Greg, who received 25% of the estate. Norman also left him his prized possession of a 1957 Chevy in his garage. Greg was a little surprised about the inheritance but did not say much, because the attorney went on to the next distribution: Marsha.

Marsha also received 25% of the estate, but her portion of the money went into a generation-skipping trust. She would only get income from her portion of the inheritance for the rest of her life. It turns out that Norman and Margaret were concerned about her current marriage. They set up a plan so, in the event of Marsha's fourth divorce, the assets would not be lost in a divorce settlement.

The next distribution was to Janet. Janet also received 25% of the estate, in addition to the vacation home in Wyoming. She received the house as a compensation for being the trustee of the estate.

Finally, the last distribution was for Peter. Like everyone else, Peter also received 25% of the estate. The only difference in Peter's inheritance was that he would collect the money over a course of fifteen years in three distribution periods. Norman and Margaret were concerned about his drinking habits. They felt, by dividing the inheritance in different periods, he would have better use for the money. The bottom line was that Norman and Margaret did not want Peter drinking it all up in one year.

After everyone received their inheritance, I received a call from Marsha to help her design a plan similar to the plan set up for Norman and Margaret. She saw how much Norman and Margaret left to their heirs and realized that she had almost nothing to retire on, much less leave to her children. I felt obligated to help her out, even though she was in another state, because I kept picturing Margaret and how concerned she was of Marsha's financial situation. It made me feel good that I could help one generation and still be there for the next. As I became familiar with Marsha's situation, I could understand why Norman and Margaret chose a generation-skipping trust. Based on the way she handled her finances, the plan was appropriate for her. Once again, Norman and Margaret's planning appeared to be solid.

Everything seemed fine for almost a year after Norman's death. Everyone was busy and back into the routine of their schedules. One day, as Janet was teaching, she noticed a strange man in a dark suit, sitting in the back of her classroom. When class ended, he came up to Janet and asked in an authoritative voice, "Are you Janet, the trustee of the Samples' trust?" Janet stood there in confusion. She had no idea who the man was or how he knew she was the trustee of the trust. She hesitantly nodded her head. The man then reached into his black leather suitcase and took out a large envelope. As he handed it to Janet, he said, "You have just been summoned." Janet nearly fainted. She managed to sit down on a student's desk and opened the envelope. Her stomach turned upside down. She was in complete shock and could not imagine who could be suing her. She simply could not believe what was happening. When she glanced at the paper, she realized that Greg filed a lawsuit against her for an ungodly amount of money. She was absolutely devastated.

Within hours, I received a frantic phone call from Janet. I was shocked about the news. Throughout my career as a financial planner, I never experienced such a lawsuit. Janet and I immediately contacted the attorney for the trust. The three of us sat down to review the summons and to discuss the basis of the lawsuit. From the way Norman and Margaret had set up the trust, if anyone challenged the language of the trust, then they would only receive $1 of the settlement. The terms of the trust were laid out so well that they were indisputable. Norman and Margaret made their wishes very clear. To our surprise, Greg did not challenge the language of the trust, he was suing Janet on the grounds that she was a bad trustee. His lawsuit was based on how the trust was managed, for instance, how the money was invested and how the money was spent.

Greg challenged Janet's management in a number of areas. First of all, Greg was furious about paying the estate taxes when Norman died. He wanted to know why nothing was done to protect the estate against taxes and blamed Janet that they had to pay taxes. Greg was also very upset that he had to pay income tax on his part of the inheritance. He did not understand that annuities were fully taxable to the beneficiaries. He did not think it was fair to pay even more taxes on the inheritance he received. Greg was very angry and bitter about the taxes. Furthermore, Greg questioned why the investments were invested so conservatively in mutual funds and annuities. He wanted to know why he was getting so little return on the investments. He felt that the investments should be making at least 20-30% more, which meant a lot more money for him. The bottom line was that Greg felt entitled to a lot of money he did not get. He was bitter and greedy about Norman's inheritance.

I was shocked at the whole procedure of an inheritance lawsuit when the case was brought to court in front of a judge. First of all, the judge appointed an accountant known as a court-appointed referee. The referee was positioned to determine whether proper accounting was followed through the Samples' trust. Proper accounting meant that every monetary transaction, such as a check, deposit, or withdrawal, had to be accounted, starting from the death of the first spouse. The reason is that the living trust technically becomes irrevocable as soon as the first spouse dies. In the Samples' case, every penny had to be scrutinized from the time of Margaret's death, which was approximately three years before Norman's death. I was astonished at this, because it was a long period of time to be keeping detailed records. There were so many transactions during that time that it took several months to accumulate the information for proper accounting.

The results of the proper accounting showed a large amount of cash withdrawals from the account for a long period of time. The large amount was due to Janet getting money for Norman to help him maintain his lifestyle when he was unable to get around. As I mentioned earlier, Norman was an individual who dealt with everything on a cash basis and never kept detailed records. When he needed money, he would call up Janet and ask her to withdraw money for him. And without question, Janet would simply go to the bank to get Norman money for his expenses. With all the unexplained cash flow, Greg could not help attack it.

Greg argued that that large amount withdrawn from the account was proof Janet was stealing money from the account. Everyone was shocked at Greg's claim. Janet was truly disappointed that anyone would make such claims about her. She could never imagine stealing money from anyone, especially her family. Greg even argued that Janet stole so much money that she was able to purchase a house with the money. But after some research, it turned out Janet had actually bought her house three years before she took over as trustee. Greg was using the old trick that if you sling enough mud, some of it is bound to stick. It is such a burden for the accused in a lawsuit to always have to prove themselves innocent. As I recall, it should be innocent until proven guilty.

Besides the money withdrawn from the account, Janet also had to explain why the money was invested so conservatively. She argued that when she took over the management of the trust, she did not want to deal with losing any of Norman's money due to poor investment decisions. Consequently, she left in place the investment structure that Norman had set up, which was a low risk/low return.

Greg did not understand Norman's mentality. Norman felt that since he and Margaret were retired, they needed safe investments that would give them a steady cash flow. Norman was non-trusting of financial institutions in general. For example, after Norman passed away, Janet went through his house to inventory everything. While going through some books, she happened upon some treasury certificates stuffed between them. This caused Janet to realize that Norman and Margaret probably had more throughout the house. She ended up finding cash, gold coins, and even stock certificates all over the house. Norman even stuffed stock certificates between record albums. They hid their money, literally, under the mattress. Janet could not believe it. She realized Norman distrusted the banking system so much that he had become his own bank!

Consequently, Norman invested mainly in very safe investments. The problem was the low rate of return they received.

This was not troublesome to Norman and Margaret, because they wanted safety above all else. When Janet became the trustee, she did not change anything, because she knew it was Norman's money and did not want to do anything Norman would disapprove of. But Greg felt Janet was not investing for maximum return, and was thus a poor trustee. He felt that if she had invested for more return, he would have received a greater inheritance.

Another issue Janet had difficulty defending was why she had brought in Chris to watch Norman, instead of taking him to a nursing home. Greg claimed that since Chris was a relative of Janet, she was benefiting from her position as trustee. He argued that Chris did not have any certification and was not qualified to watch Norman. The simple fact was that Norman did not require a nursing home at that time. Janet was able to rationalize the lack of certification because Chris was a family member and would take good care of Norman. Norman needed a companion and someone to keep him company and out of trouble. As you know, Norman strongly disliked nursing homes and did not want to go until it was no longer possible for him to take care of himself.

In the meantime, Marsha's husband, Sam, decided to lend a helping hand to Greg. He wrote letters and did all he could to support Greg in the lawsuit. Janet's brother, Peter, also decided to lend a helping hand to Greg. He got access to Janet's account and found out how much money she had. Janet was absolutely crushed. At that time, she needed their support, not more issues to deal with. Peter and Sam were now doing everything they could to get more money. Peter even called Janet to warn her that if she was going to mess with his money, then he was going to mess her up. Janet couldn't believe that her own brother would personally threaten her. Janet was very upset after the phone call. As she hung up the phone with Peter, she knew things would never be the same again.

The lawsuit was in court for over three years. In addition, the cost of the accounting alone was over $12,000. The estate was eaten away with court costs, accounting fees, and lawyer expenses. All the beneficiaries of the trust all had to pay from some of their recent inheritance to cover all of the fees involved in the lawsuit. The heirs each gave up roughly 10 to 15% of their inheritance for this lawsuit. The court did not find in favor of either party and reached a compromise between the two. Janet had to pay penalties of about $35,000 for not keeping a proper accounting of the trust. Janet was upset at the settlement because she still felt she had done nothing wrong as a trustee. The fines felt like an insult because she went through so much and was punished for it in the end. But her attorney advised her to settle because the case had dragged on for so long. Greg was also disappointed in the settlement because he ended up losing money. Greg's so upset that he's now suing his lawyer. No one ended up winning the case except, of course, the lawyers involved.

Janet called me when the case closed. She expressed regret over the whole affair, and now considers herself an only child.

When I asked her if she would ever be a trustee again, she immediately replied, "No way…. There is not a chance." It disturbed me that Janet felt this way. But she explained that she was happy we did so much planning on Norman and Margaret's behalf. Janet continued to explain that the trust "was like an iron ship around me and it took a lot of hits. . . and it stood up. In the end it stood up, and I was able to do everything for Norman." It was such a shame that greed can cause such hard feelings within a family. She even said, "To think if I went into this with no trust…. Norman would have been dead years before." She felt the other relatives would have let him die to get the inheritance.

She referred back to the time when Norman was complaining of a hurt hip. Janet took him to a doctor who examined him and found several problems, including the onset of pneumonia and swelling, especially in the ankles. The doctor told her that he could prescribe something, or "if we just let it go, in two days he'll be gone." It turned out the cost of the medication was $8. The doctor was willing to let Norman go for $8. At that point, Norman was still able to hold conversations and get around on his own. Janet felt certain other relatives might have chosen to let Norman go.

Even though Janet would never take on the responsibilities of a trustee again, she explained she would still care for Norman if she could. Some people consider taking care of Norman a full-time job, but Janet described it as part of her day. "If your child is sick, you don't look at that as a chore. It was the same way with Norman."

There are many lessons to learn from this case. Some of the seven most common mistakes that I came up with that trustees often make are based from this case. Obviously, there are more mistakes out there, but from my experience, these seven seem to be the most common. I truly believe that if you pay attention to the details covered by these seven mistakes, you will greatly reduce your chances of a lawsuit in the future.

Mistake #1
Failure to Communicate

Norman tried to discuss the details of their decision to have Janet become the trustee with her. Because Janet refused to have the discussion (it made her uncomfortable to think about her parents dying and she had no clear idea of what a trustee was), Norman put it off. This also meant that none of the other beneficiaries was informed about who would be the trustee until Janet took over. Sometimes it can help if the trustors (generally the parents) tell the beneficiaries whom they have selected and why. It may also be helpful to discuss distribution plans in advance so there are no surprises.

Failing to communicate properly with all parties involved with the trust is perhaps the biggest mistake trustees make. There are many levels of miscommunications that trustees must face. From my experience, parents must deal with two important predicaments before considering advanced planning. But the predicaments cannot be resolved without first establishing proper communication. I have also found that once planning takes place, children must also face predicaments of their own. The way children work through their own predicaments depends greatly on communication within the family. Through my experience, families that avoid Mistake #1 have a foundation that is able to withstand almost any type of problem in the future.

Parents' Predicament #1:

Do we have enough money
to last us the rest of our lives?

Oftentimes, parents do not want to give away too much of their money for fear they will not have enough to live on for themselves. No one knows how long he or she will live. Each year the average life-span of Americans increases. In fact, the largest growing age bracket is senior citizens. As of 1999, over 70,000 people in the US were over the age of 100. Can you imagine being 75 years old and thinking that your time is coming to an end, and then living another 25 years? Just last year, a European woman passed away at the age of 125. This woman was born in the 1800's and saw almost the entire 20th century. Almost everything your children studied in history class, like the two World Wars, this lady lived through. The effects of modern medicine, diet and exercise increases longevity, and people are living longer all the time. During one of my seminars, someone told me that the oldest person is still alive at the age of 137. I'm not sure if this is true, but it shows that you need to plan ahead for your future well in advance. People need to realize that staying alive costs lots of money. Just because people are living older does not mean they are always mentally and physically able to handle things. More and more people are living in nursing homes because they cannot take care of themselves.

With all this to be aware of, if there is not enough money to last you for the rest of your life, then financial planning needs to be developed before estate planning can take place. Estate planning is not even an issue at this point. But on the other hand, if there is enough money, the next predicament of estate planning can be achieved.

Parents' Predicament #2:
Do I want my spouse to know all the financial details of the estate?

The next predicament people have to face is whether they want their spouses to know where all their assets are. From my experience, one spouse, usually the husband, handles the finances, while the other knows very little about them. But what often happens is that one day the husband dies and the wife is suddenly overwhelmed because she doesn't know what to do with the finances, where to go for advice, where the investments are, or how the investments have been doing. Most people do not realize that, within nine months of the death of the first spouse, the IRS requires the surviving family to file and separate the AB trust. Usually by the 7th or 8th month, the bereaved widow is rushing around trying to figure out what to do with the money. During this critical period, I've seen new widows being taken advantage of because they're forced to seek advice wherever they can find it. She can easily become a victim to someone who might not have her best interests in mind.

Planning before tragedy strikes is important, but communicating during planning is even more important. There are many opportunities that exist if everyone works together to maximize the investment. For instance, when both spouses are still alive, the IRS allows unlimited transfers of assets between spouses. This is a tremendous planning tool, because assets can be positioned to eliminate or minimize estate taxes. The privilege is immediately lost upon the death of the first spouse, so if proper estate planning has not been implemented, it becomes much more difficult to reduce the burden of estate taxes. Just remember that if you fail to plan, then you plan to fail. Estate planning alone can save thousands of dollars in estate taxes.

During this time, couples need to work together to establish financial goals and decide what they must plan for, for example, a child's education or retirement. It is crucial that husbands and wives communicate with each other their true feelings and desires. It is especially important in 2nd or 3rd marriages, so spouses can determine where they want to allocate their money without problems in the future.

— ·· — · — ·· — · — ·· — · — ·· — · — ·· — ·· —

Case Study #1:
Planning without spouse communication

Communication within the family is so essential during planning. My client, Bill, for example, discovered the importance of it the hard way. I met Bill when he attended one of my seminars on estate planning. At my seminar, Bill sat quietly by himself. He appeared to be in deep thought through-out the entire presentation. Bill was an engineer at a local company in San Diego. He was a very analytical person and planned everything in great detail. In fact, when Bill was 48, he planned exactly how much he needed for retirement. Bill felt he knew how to do everything, so he did not consult any financial professionals. He just used sources from the Inter-net. But after attending one of my seminars, Bill made an appointment to meet with me at my office.

When I meet a client for the first time in my office, I usually start out by asking them a few questions and taking some notes. But I'll never forget my first meeting with Bill. As soon as Bill sat down, he placed his brown leather brief-case on my desk and pulled out an old newspaper article. He briefly glanced at the article and passed it across the desk. No words were exchanged. I was very eager what Bill wanted to show me. I looked over at him with curiosity and picked up the article. I started reading the newspaper clipping and realized it was an article about a head-on car accident. On the right-hand side of the article, there was a picture of an arm hanging out of the window of a crushed vehicle. I glanced up at Bill and he quietly said, "That's my wife."

He continued to explain that she was killed in a car accident about six months ago. He broke into tears as talked about his wife. Then he told me about the plan he had cre-ated for their future. Bill had created an elaborate plan for his wife after he would pass away. He wanted to make sure she had nothing to worry about and covered every aspect of her life after his death. But Bill had not considered one major thing: his wife died first.

Bill worked long hours and didn't realize exactly what his wife did around the house. When his wife died, Bill did not know how to handle all the daily living duties, such as cooking and cleaning. Truthfully, he had no desire to learn.

His wife's death really changed his whole life. He had to re-plan his entire future.

Bill was a very smart man and tried to develop a detailed plan for his future on his own. Unfortunately, he overlooked several components. But his story illustrates that when it comes to estate planning—no matter how much you try to do on your own—you need experienced advisors to help you realize all the hypothetical situations that may take place. Anything can happen; so it's important to communicate not just on financial issues, but also everyday issues.

Parents' Predicament #3:

Do we want our children to know
the financial details of the estate?

Parents are concerned that if they tell the children about their finances, then the children might act differently toward them. For instance, parents are concerned that if they tell the children everything, then the children will now start thinking of the money as theirs. These are big concerns because if there is a big inheritance coming in the future, do they have a reason to start looking over their shoulders?

But on the flip side, parents often contemplate whether informing their children of the inheritance would do more good than bad to the child. They fear creating a "trust junkie" that would kill the child's motivation to make something important out of their lives.

It's tempting for a child to meander through life knowing there is a steady supply of money. But not all children are like that. It's important to look at your children and determine their capability of handling finances. Norman and Margaret Sample, for instance, did excellent planning in this area. They realized Marsha was in her fourth marriage and had financial problems. As a result, Marsha's inheritance was in a generation-skipping trust, because Norman and Margaret did not want her losing the money in another divorce settlement. Norman and Margaret also did an excellent job spending time and carefully picking their successor trustee for the estate. They picked someone who was responsible and financially mature. In the end, Janet was the best trustee for the estate, despite all the problems with the greedy relatives.

From my experience, I find that the same parents who do not want to tell their children anything about their finances suddenly want to tell them everything once they experience something life-threatening, such as being diagnosed with cancer or having a stroke or heart attack. Their attitude then changes like night to day. They suddenly realize that all the finances need to be in order before they pass on.

— — — — — — — — — — —

Case Study #2:

Children who know too much about their parents' finances

My clients, Nathaniel and Cynthia Spencer, are very hardworking people. Together they raised two sons in their home in San Diego. The oldest son, Andrew, is very much like his father, with simple, strong values. Andrew lives in

Irvine with his wife and four children. The youngest son, Daniel, did not possess the same qualities as his father. His father described him as more of a "get-rich-quick" type of person, because he was never really interested in hard work. In fact, Daniel moved to Chicago to have a fast-paced life. He now lives there with his wife and four children.

Nathaniel and Cynthia are both in their late 70's and financially well off, because Nathaniel worked for the same company, Johnson & Johnson, his whole life. Through their investment plan, Nathaniel was able to accumulate a large estate (about $2 million) with Johnson & Johnson stock. He accumulated quite a bit of capital gains after holding the stock for so long.

About a year before I met Nathaniel, he decided he should start planning for the future. Nathaniel was a quick learner when it came to estate planning and felt he could handle the job. He attended a few seminars and attempted some "do-it-yourself" financial planning. He was aware of the personal exclusion from estate taxes and decided it would be a good thing to let his children have some of his wealth while he was still alive. He decided to use then the personal exclusion of $600,000 to do it.

Nathaniel needed help with all the legal paperwork, so he contacted his neighbor's daughter. The daughter worked for a local law firm and, although she was not an estate planning attorney, agreed to draw up the documents necessary to accomplish Nathaniel's goals. Nathaniel gave a gift of $300,000 of his stock to his heirs. He gave $100,000 to each son and spilt the remaining $100,000 among his grandchildren. He used part of his lifetime exclusion in order to beat the gift. The attorney did not raise any objections to anything Nathaniel did.

A few months later, Daniel's friend, who was a commodities broker, told him he could make a killing in the commodities market. When Daniel heard about all the money he would make, he became very interested. But Daniel was not dumb. He knew that if he sold the stock his father had given him, the capital gains would take away a good portion of the money. So, instead, he put the stock into a margin account, where he could borrow against it to invest in commodities. But a few weeks later, Daniel found out that his friend was a better salesman than analyst. The money quickly went away along with a recent downturn in the commodities market. The loss in value of the commodities triggered a margin call, which forced Daniel to sell off some of his shares of stock. In addition, he had to pay the capital gains tax on the stock that he sold off, which meant that he had to sell off even more shares.

When Nathaniel heard what Daniel did, he was furious. Nathaniel went to Chicago to straighten everything out. Daniel told his father that lately he was doing some reading on estate planning and it was in his father's best interest to go ahead and gift to him up to the full exclusion limit. The bottom line was that Daniel basically needed more money and knew where to turn. He was aware his father was able to give him a large sum of money without affecting his own standard of living. It was then that Nathaniel decided he needed professional financial advice. He knew what was going on.

Nathaniel came to me and admitted he needed help with estate planning. He explained his complicated situation with his money and his son. After some analysis, I recommended to him a capital gains bypass trust. I explained in full detail that with the help of charities and insurance, both capital gains and death tax would be eliminated and, in the end, even his beneficiaries would receive more money.

Nathaniel's eyes opened in amazement as I told him more about the capital gains bypass trust. Nathaniel was very pleased with our arrangement. It was the first time he realized what true financial planning was. He realized that financial planning was not just buying and selling stock. After my meeting, Nathaniel understood the value of competent advisors, as well as the importance of communication with his sons.

Children's Predicament #1:

I don't feel I should interfere with my parents' finances.

From my experience, I find that when parents finally decide to tell the children about their assets, the children usually face two predicaments. First of all, children do not know how to deal with trust arrangements. For instance, when the Samples' first told Janet about the trust, she did not even know what a trust was. To her, it had a negative connotation of death. She did not even want to talk about the trust. She told Norman and Margaret that it was their money and they were going to be around for several years. Children react like Janet for many reasons. They do not want to talk about their parents dying, or possibly going to a nursing home. The simple reason is because it involves death, specifically the deaths of their parents.

Children's Predicament #2:

If I take an interest, will I be perceived as being greedy?

At the same time, children feel they have to act like they don't care about the trust, because if they seem too interested in the money, they will be perceived as greedy. If the children take an active role in their parents' finances, they worry about how they will be perceived by their parents and their brothers and sisters. The truth is children need to approach their parents on estate planning if the parents do not discuss it. Children need to know what their parents want to accomplish with their finances after they are gone, because everything needs to be taken care of before it's too late. Because finances can be a touchy subject, it might help to discuss the goals rather than the actual figures of the estate. It's amazing how much can be accomplished if both parties work towards both the parents' and children's goals.

My successor trustee is a bank—did I made the right decision?

From my experience, I have often seen people use third parties or financial institutions as their successor trustee as a way to deal with the communication problems. I cannot tell you how many times my clients ask me to become the trustee of their estate. I've turned them down every single time, because I consider myself a family advisor and advise my clients on how to manage their estate. People sometimes take the easy way out and give the power of attorney to financial institutions, like banks. In my experience, involvement of a third party causes lots of problems within the estate in the long run. In each of the scenarios that I've been involved with, the children were left thinking after the parents passed away, "Why did Mom and Dad not trust us with this responsibility?" Furthermore, the children ended up disagreeing with the banks or third parties. I found that third parties, such as banks, do not always look out for the best interest of the trust. Sometimes their investments have not performed up to market. It's mostly because banks are required to use their own institution's investments. For example, I knew a lady named Alice who left her local bank as the successor trustee of her estate instead of her daughter. When Alice passed away, the first thing the bank did was liquidate all her stocks and put all the assets in the bank's money market accounts. Honestly, there was no reason for liquidating the stocks, because they were doing very well. The bank also did not realize it would trigger a large capital gain. For obvious reasons, Alice's daughter became very upset. I don't think that Alice or her daughter realized the bank would make such harsh decisions about her estate. Personally, I believe if you're going to leave money for the beneficiaries, the best way is to communicate and let them know your goals and objectives.

It's important to realize that estate planning and financial planning are two entirely different issues. Financial planning involves making money. It is constantly changing and takes a time frame of five to ten years time. Remember that making money is only half the battle. Estate planning deals with how to keep the money and pass it on to succeeding generations. It includes protection against you and your trustee's losses (such as taxation, creditors, bankruptcy, divorces, accident, premature death, substance abuse). A good time frame on good solid estate planning is about 100 years and lasts for several generations. Only with proper communication can you achieve solid estate planning for the next 100 years.

Mistake #2
Failure to Hire the Appropriate Advisors

Janet fired her parents' financial advisor and moved all of Norman's invest-ments into low risk CDs and fixed annuities at a bank where she felt comfort-able. She did not seek professional legal or tax advice.

In the last decade, tremendous changes have taken place in the area of estate planning. Estate planning is a growing sec-tor that is becoming more complex with its constant changes. Every year laws are revised and added. When it comes to making important financial decisions, it's important you con-sult professionals for appropriate advice.

The appropriate advisors are made up of attorneys, accoun-tants, and financial planners. In today's changing times, the individual roles of these groups are evolving. For instance, the financial advisor is not only doing investments but also selling insurance. In estate planning, many attorneys as well as CPAs are expanding their roles and getting involved with the financial aspects of planning.

When I meet with potential clients, I often ask them who are their current advisors. They usually think about it for awhile and say something like, "Well, my tax person for the last couple years has saved me from several audits. So he's my accountant. And since I've never been sued, I don't really have a lawyer. But I attended some seminars on living trusts and this person set up my trust, so I suppose he's my attorney. My financial planner? Well, now that I'm retired, I manage my own assets with my resources on the Internet, so I'm my own financial planner."

This arrangement is great for financial planning, but when it comes to estate planning, it is not a team approach. Estate planning involves you being the chariot driver of three horses. Since you are in control of the horses, you cannot drive and be a horse at the same time. Because the minute the driver is thrown from the chariot, the three horses tend to run wild in three different directions.

I can't tell you how many cases I've been involved in when a death has taken place and the widow spouse is overwhelmed with different advice from the different advisors. The first thing all the advisors (the accountant, attorney and financial advisor) fight for is control from the client. The reason is when the other spouse was still alive, the spouse made all the decisions. Now that the spouse is gone, the advisors want to be in charge. I cannot even describe the chaos this causes for the surviving widow, simply because there is no game plan. Most of the time, the advisors never knew about each other's position. But when a death takes place, oftentimes the attorney needs to file some legal documents that require issues regarding taxes and finances. It all becomes very confusing, especially when there is no set plan and the advisors are unaware of each other's roles. Because of all this, it is very important to hire appropriate advisors. Advisors should be brought in together so that they can work as a team. Chances are, if they have worked together in the past and have a solid relationship, then the team will work well. They will know each other's strengths and know how to complement one another.

The best way to think of the relationship between your advisors is to imagine a three-legged stool. Each leg represents your accountant, attorney and financial advisor. You can even represent yourself as an advisor. But imagine upon your death if one of those legs becomes weak and collapses. Does the stool collapse as well? Immediately. It's up to the remaining people to put all the pieces back together. Sometimes the people do it right, sometimes they do it wrong. After a lot of problems, hindsight is then clear. Heirs, or the next occupant of the stool, often ask, "Why didn't they plan it the right way? Why didn't Mom and Dad talk to me about this?" Sadly enough, I've heard this complaint far too many times.

—·—·—·—·—·—·—·—·—·—·—·—·—

What do you look for in an advisor?

In order to develop a good estate plan strategy, your advisors need to know these following areas:

     1.   The current laws that will affect your estate and the options available to protect the estate from being reduced,

     2.   How to reduce and eliminate your taxes on your estate, and

     3.   How to take advantage of your investment options to maximize your assets.

It is impossible for any one advisor to stay on top of all of these areas. Each area is specialized and complex. Your advisors at least need to be aware of the current and future laws in their area.

— ·—·—·—·—·—·—·—·—·—·—·—

Attorneys

When looking for a lawyer, the most important thing to look out for is experience in estate planning. If the attorney working on your estate plan is the same attorney that set up your business and handles your legal problems, you may want to find a more specialized lawyer. Estate planning involves complicated issues. These issues can be overlooked and ignored by someone not familiar with this area.

Be careful in your search for a good lawyer and do not go blindly into a new relationship. Unfortunately, there are some lawyers out there who make decisions based on how it will affect their pocketbook. It is important to educate yourself as much as possible about the options available. Ask the new attorney the questions provided in Appendix A. Another good way to learn about your lawyer is through their previous clients. Any mistakes made now will not show up until there is trouble, and usually by then it is too late.

— ·—·—·—·—·—·—·—·—·—·—·—

Accountants

When searching for a competent accountant, be aware of their job function. The main function of an accountant is to evaluate the income and expenditures, and minimize the amount of taxes that you owe to the government. It is not extremely difficult to find an accountant that can do this adequately. The difficulty is finding one that will look into the future and make recommendations to help you save taxes in the future.

When looking for an accountant, experience is once again very important in matters of estate planning. They should know current and even pending laws, because they could affect your estate. Furthermore, your accountant must be willing to develop strategies with you that will minimize your future taxes. If not, at least they must be willing to be open-minded about ideas and strategies given to you by your other advisors. Far too often, accountants get into a routine and are unwilling to even consider alternative tax-saving strategies. They cannot see ahead into the future for the obvious traps set for their clients down the road.

—·—·—·—·—·—·—·—·—·—·—·—·—

Financial Advisors

Advisors are probably a good idea in every case, because they can come up with new ideas the family might have overlooked. The advisor can encourage communication between spouses that can help determine goals for their future. But most importantly, having an advisor allows someone outside the family to know every aspect of the situation. It is especially helpful because, when one of the spouse passes away, the surviving spouse has someone they already know and trust to turn to for advice.

Your financial advisor coordinates the activities that relate to your estate plan. But be aware there are many types of financial advisors out there. If your investment advisor is the same gentleman who has been giving you recommendations for your stock portfolio for 25 years, you might want to consider looking elsewhere for an estate-planning advisor. I do not suggest you end the former relationship, but estate planning may not be their area of expertise. Even though your financial planner can only advise you, with proper advice you can make extraordinary decisions. Once again, experience is an important factor of proper estate planning.

Previously I discussed the differences between an adequate estate plan and "super" planning. You must decide what type of planning you want to do. Some people are content with not planning at all. They figure their parents and grandparents did not leave them anything, so why should they leave anything for their children? If that is truly the way you feel, then there is nothing I can say or do to convince you otherwise. But once you realize that with the proper planning from the right advisors you can leave your children all of your money instead of making them split it with the government, you might think, your heirs deserve your hard-earned money. If you put off the decision, it will be made for you. Procrastination is a choice in itself.

Whether or not to use proper advisors is similar to the idea of building a house. You can go out and build your own house with just a little knowledge about how to make it look good enough to live in. It would even be adequate for comfortable living in comfortable times. The true test is when a storm hits. If the house is constructed well, it will withstand the storm. Even if it looks good on the surface but is hiding many small mistakes, it will fall apart with a little pressure. The true test of financial planning is not in good times. The true test of the quality of your financial plans are when the times are tough. Unfortunately at this point, mistakes might be too late to correct. But if you surround yourself with good advisors, you can dramatically reduce your chances of making a mistake. Small mistakes now can have drastic effects after you are gone.

Examples

Jim Austin – The Importance of Communication Among the Advisors

Jim's mother, Thelma, built up a reasonably large estate throughout her life. In fact, she was worth over $600,000, including her home. In the early eighties, Jim noticed that Thelma was unable to take care of herself like she should. Jim, being her only child, decided it was time to check his mother into a nursing home. Unfortunately, she did not have long-term care insurance, so the nursing home was paid out of her estate.

Jim decided to sell his mother's house first and use the proceeds to pay for her care in the nursing home. A few years went by and soon all of this money was used up. The nursing home increased its expenses every year, so Thelma's money went that much more quickly. Jim then started liquidating Thelma's stock.

Thelma had owned it for so long that it had some fairly sizable capital gains. When Jim sold the stock, he had to pay capital gains, and then pay the nursing home. In reality, the nursing home was costing him more because of this extra tax.

Jim had an accountant handle his mother's taxes, but it was not the accountant's responsibility to recommend alternative strategies to Jim. This process of liquidating stock and paying the capital gains went on for several years.

When I met Jim a few years ago, he was desperate. His mother was still going strong, after over ten years in the nursing home, but her estate was down to about $100,000. Jim was afraid that the money would run out and he would have to start using his own money to pay for his mother's care. He was a public school teacher and did not make much.

Once I looked at the whole situation and had a grasp on what had been going on, I was able to reposition Thelma's assets. At that point, she was able to qualify for MediCal from the State of California. This paid for her stay in the nursing home and, consequently slowed down the depletion of Thelma's estate. Now Jim was able to use her money for any incidental items she needed, and it virtually guaranteed the money would last until she died.

I would like to point out that Medicare does not cover long-term care. This cost must come out of your pocket until you have almost nothing left. At this point, you can usually qualify for some form of assistance, based on need, from the government. In the State of California, this is called MediCal. This differs from state to state, and you should check with your state government for the rules regarding qualification in your state.

—·—·—·—·—·—·—·—·—·—·—·—·—

William Grider – Use Proper Advisors Before It's Too Late

Since William Grider was a very good corporate attorney, he felt he did not need outside assistance when it came to developing an estate plan for his mother. He took care of her needs in the estate planning process, even though this was not his area of expertise. He figured he could save a few dollars by doing the job himself and not seeking the proper team of advisors.

William's mother died just under nine months before I first met with him. At that time, he decided it might be a good idea to get a financial advisor on his side. Unfortunately, it was really too late to help him with his mother's estate. He ended up writing a check to the IRS from his mother's estate for a total of $1.5 million. If the proper planning had been done ahead of time, he could have held on to almost all of this money. It's just a shame that so many people do not realize they need help until it is too late.

—·—·—·—·—·—·—·—·—·—·—·—·—

Dr. John Fischer – Life Insurance With a Long-term Outlook

Dr. John Fischer was a head-strong, do-it-yourself kind of guy, who did not believe in asking or receiving help from others. He would rather just push his way through, even if he's not quite sure what he is doing. His financial affairs were no exception.

John, 57, has a wife and three children. His children range in age from 13 to 22. His wife did not work because John made a very good living. In fact, John was worth about a million dollars. They had a rather expensive house that was still being paid for, so they relied quite heavily on John's salary.

About twenty years ago, John decided that he needed to provide for his family in case he should die prematurely. He thought he knew all there was to know about life insurance, so he shopped around and looked for the best deal. He found the least expensive alternative, his choice: term insurance. He was right. When he compared all the many different types of insurance, term was definitely the cheapest. After all, he was thirty-five years old and in good health. So he was getting a bargain, right? Well, not really. If he only needed insurance for a short period, say a couple of years, it was perfect for his situation. Unfortunately, John needed this to last his whole life.

There are two major drawbacks to term insurance. The first is that the cost goes up every year—the older you get, the more significant these increases become. Yet, you are not building up any cash value, so if you cancel the policy before you die, you have thrown away all that money. The second major drawback is you must periodically re-qualify for this insurance policy that you have been paying on for years. If your health takes a turn for the worse, you may not be able to get insurance, just when you need it the most.

Ironically, John had quadruple bypass surgery this past spring. He survived the surgery, but I don't know if his life insurance policy is going to make it. He is currently paying around $4200 per quarter and it does not look good for continued coverage. Now if he decides to change to a more appropriate form of life insurance, he most likely will not be able to. If John had sought help from an appropriate advisor with a long-term outlook, he might not be in his current situation.

Mistake #3
Failure to Follow the UPIA

Janet did not know about, let alone follow, the statutes of the Uniform Prudent Investor Act (UPIA). This put the trust at risk and her in a position of liability.

The next mistake is more legal in nature than the previous two mistakes. It involves the UPIA, or, more specifically, the lack of knowledge of it. What's the UPIA? If you have never heard of the UPIA, let me reassure you that you are certainly in the majority. It is important to understand because it can have an enormous impact on the actions you take as trustee.

UPIA stands for Uniform Prudent Investor Act (see Appendix B). It was established in California and ten other states in 1996 to replace the Prudent Man Law. Do not ignore this new law! Ignoring this law increases your chances of being sued. It provides an easy way for a disgruntled heir and a slick lawyer to prove that a trustee is unfit to manage the trust, who will then owe significant amounts of their personal money back to the trust.

The UPIA forces a trustee to make a written plan of what to do with the assets in the trust. It calls for detailed descriptions of what will comprise the investments held by the trust. This plan must be well diversified, well documented and follow the modern portfolio theory. It must also be sufficiently risky to bring in a respectable return. An investment solely in certificates of deposit is not acceptable. These financial vehicles generally do not provide enough growth to overcome inflation, especially once taxes are taken into account. An investment, which gradually loses its purchasing power over the years, may be considered "safe" from losing principal, but in the long run can do more damage to the account than a more "risky" investment.

There are two big differences between the Prudent Man Law and the UPIA. The first difference is the strict documentation. The second difference is the standard to which the written plan is held. The Prudent Man Law was somewhat ambiguous in the trustee's definition of a "prudent man". It was left up to the judge to decide if the decisions made were "prudent". Now, the trustee and his plan are held to the same standards as a bank. The knowledge required of the trustee is the same amount of knowledge required of an institution devoted to making money. The accountability and responsibility are also the same. There is an incredible liability for a trustee. If it is determined that the investment plan was not good enough, the trustee is held accountable.

This new law also comes with a unique ability. The trustee can pass this entire burden and liability to someone else. The trustee can find a competent financial planner to handle the finances for the trust. Then the trustee can turn over all the responsibility and liability to that financial planner. The only liability the trustee now holds is his choice of a financial planner. He or she must be able to show that the planner is competent at handling this type of situation. Of course, this should not be a problem if the trustee asks the right questions up front (review Mistake #2 for more details).

One other option is that the trustor can put a statement into the trust documents that states the trust is exempt from the UPIA. If this is included in the written trust, it should hold true if tested by a disgruntled beneficiary down the road.

Trustees need to be aware that, within the UPIA, every decision is judged in hindsight. Courts look at the track record and then judge the decisions the trustee made. The trustee may not be aware of problems for a long time; by then it is too late to correct them. It is a good idea to seek other opinions before you make decisions.

———————————————————

Up to this point, the examples I've provided are from my own personal experience. I also want to share with you some experiences other estate planning professionals have dealt with. These examples will show you some horrible things that can happen to your estate, even before you pass away. These are extreme cases, but they illustrate what can happen if you are not careful.

When I talked to Jim Watts, an estate planning attorney in San Diego, about my book, I asked him what he thought was the biggest mistake a trustee could make. His reply was simple. He said the biggest mistake was accepting the job. At that time, he was laughing, but he was still making a good point.

Jim gave me some examples of actual cases to use in my book. Some stories are hard to believe, but they illustrate good points. The first example is a court case that Jim was not personally involved with, but uses as an example for his clients. It was a lawsuit taken all the way to the Supreme Court. It is known as U.S. v. Carlton (U.S. v. Carlton S.Ct.Dk. # 92-1941, 6-13-94).

In this case, Carlton was an estate-planning attorney, based in Orange County, California. He performed a detailed and comprehensive estate plan for one of his clients. He was also the trustee for the trust. He thought everything was in order.

Carlton's client passed away in 1986. Carlton performed his duties without flaw. He wrapped everything up and got a letter of closure from the IRS. This meant that all the estate taxes had been paid, and the estate was in the clear and ready to be distributed to the heirs. The heirs were ready to receive their inheritance, and Carlton was cleared with the IRS to give them their inheritance. So he did. He distributed all the assets in the trust to all of the heirs. Case closed.

The following year, 1987, Congress passed a law that changed the tax code. That is fine; they can do that. However, they made it retroactive to the last quarter of the previous year. This changed things a bit, specifically it changed the way Carlton's client's estate would be handled by the IRS. The ever-efficient IRS sent Carlton a tax bill for that estate in the amount of

$680,000. Since Carlton was the trustee for the trust, he was PERSONALLY responsible for that money.

Remember that the IRS had considered the case closed just a few months before. Now they demanded this new tax payment, based on changes Congress made after the fact. It just does not seem right. It didn't to Carlton either, so he challenged it in court. It went all the way to the Supreme Court. They found that it stood, and Carlton was liable for the tax bill. It is also a good time to note the date on the case—1994. Anytime courts are involved, there is going to be a long waiting period. If the beneficiaries have not yet received their inheritance, litigation just puts it off a little longer.

In addition, ever since grade school we have been taught that if you do something and later that something is made illegal, you cannot be tried for it. In legal terms this is called ex post facto. This still holds true, but only refers to criminal acts. Civil acts do not fall into the same category. Congress has the ability to change the law—any civil law—and make it retroactive. It's difficult to plan for things when you do not know what the future holds.

Mistake #4
Failure to Follow Terms of the Trust

This one is not specifically related to anyone in this story. However, it is a major mistake trustees need to avoid.

The most important part of estate planning is the trust. It seems obvious, but surprisingly I have seen a lack of planning and knowledge over this subject. The trust is something that should not be taken lightly. It must be well thought out and written to express your exact desires. There can be no ambiguity in a trust. There can also be no assumption that your heirs will know what your intentions are. You must be as specific as possible when writing this document.

"Follow the Terms of the Trust" refers to the actual language in the trust. Most people do not fully understand exactly what is communicated in their trust. It is important that you have someone explain these areas to you. If you have an experienced attorney set up the trust, then they can design a trust for you that communicates your desires. Unfortunately, when people set up a trust, they look for the lowest cost.

In San Diego, I have seen the cost of a simple husband-and-wife living trust range anywhere from $125 to $3500. There is a big difference between those two prices. As far as the length of the trust, I have seen one as thin as seven pages and as thick as 100 pages or more. Both of these trusts avoid probate. They also give the marital deduction and power of attorney. The important thing to remember is that this document needs to speak when you are unable to. When this document is read, it needs to express your every desire for your estate after you are gone. If the seven-page version can do this for you, then it might be the right one for you. Be careful, though, because there may be several things that you may have left out.

Many lawyers offer what I call "cookie-cutter" trusts for a low amount of money. These trusts do not offer the uniqueness required in most cases. In these types of trusts, the lawyer has a standard form and just goes through and changes the names on the trust. You basically get what you pay for.

For example, one of my clients met with an attorney to set up a trust. They chose this attorney because he offered the cheapest trust they could find. They sat down with him and gave all of the relevant information. He took this information and in a couple of days called them back into his office to go over the trust. They did not spend much time looking it over in his office, but took it home, promising to go through it. Luckily, they did actually read through it and found several people named in the trust they had never heard of. They made another appointment with the lawyer to ask him about the names. When they pointed this out to him, he reluctantly admitted these were people named in a previous trust he had set up. He had forgotten to change the names. Imagine the confusion if these clients had never bothered to read through the trust and accepted it blindly. When they passed away, there would have been an enormous mess. Of course, I'm sure a lawyer could have straightened it out for their heirs, for a slight fee.

Your attorney determines the terms of the trust. You must review them carefully and decide whether he accurately expresses what you want to say. If you buy a cookie-cutter trust, there is no way to express your individual ideas and desires.

Your first big step in preparing a trust is to determine exactly what you want your trust to say. You need to ask your lawyer certain questions to help you figure out your needs, and you need to think about these questions before you talk to him. Most people go to a trust lawyer for the first time and the lawyer will ask what they want their trust to say. The most typical reply is that they want what everybody else has. Either that, or they will ask the lawyer what he thinks they should do.

These are decisions that are going to stand when you die. It is a simple matter that requires thought. Unfortunately, they cannot be changed after you pass on. It is so important to actually think about these decisions before you sit down in front of a lawyer and answer his or her questions. To help you get going with this, I provided some things to think about in Appendix C.

If there is a dispute over your estate, the first thing that anyone involved in the case is going to ask for is a copy of the trust. Any lawyer, judge, accountant or court official is going to read this. At this point, if there is any ambiguity in your trust, it will be evident to everyone. This ambiguity will make it much easier for a greedy individual to get to your money. Everyone is bound by the language of the trust. It is a very important document. I cannot emphasize this enough. The trust basically says everything you need to say when you are not around to argue your point. You and your lawyer should cover all the bases, or your heirs could suffer in the future.

Congratulations, if you have already set up a trust! You have taken the first step. Now you need to make sure the trust communicates what you want it to communicate. You have the ability to do so, but if you do not use it, it is worthless.

As a trustee, it is very important to follow the terms of the trust established by the trustor. You must know exactly the language of the trust. You must also be able to interpret what the trustor wanted to say. It is important to review the trust with the trustor and the lawyer long before you need to take over. You must understand what is expected of you, and know the plan of action when it is your time to take over.

If you are the trustor, you must decide how you want small items divided up amongst your heirs. Parents may want to leave a certain item to one particular child. If these wishes are not written out in the trust, it can become a disputable item. If you do not care who gets a particular item, you still need to establish a pecking order for your heirs. This gives them a guideline on who gets first pick. Luckily, this is easy to do. Just decide whether the order is oldest to youngest, or if they all draw names out of a hat. Either way, it does not matter, as long as you decide it for them before you die. It will save arguments later.

Once a death has taken place, it is too late at that point to insert the wishes of the deceased. The main reason the language of the trust is indisputable is the fact that in most trusts there is a line which states that any beneficiary who challenges the language of the trust automatically gets only $1. In the Sample case, Greg did not challenge the wording of the trust, because he could have lost everything. Instead, he challenged all the actions Janet took after becoming the trustee. This was much easier to challenge, and he actually had a good shot at winning.

Appendix D provides a list of common terminology involved with trusts.

_._._._._._._._._._._._._._._._

Examples

The following example is provided by Jim Watts. It is another court case that Jim uses to show his clients mistakes in estate planning.

This case involved an attorney who did not word the trust he set up properly. In fact, he added one word that he should not have. This one word changed the whole meaning of the trust in the eyes of the IRS.

The attorney's client wanted to set up a typical AB Trust. For those unfamiliar with this terminology, it allows the deceased's spouse to use their estate tax exclusion upon death. In fact, it doubles the amount of assets exempt from estate taxes upon the death of the second spouse.

When the first spouse dies, his or her assets go into a trust that has a limited access by the surviving spouse. Basically, the surviving spouse can receive the interest earned by investments within the trust. They can get to the principal only for a certain reason. There are four reasons acceptable by the IRS for a spouse to withdraw the principal. They are health, education, support and maintenance. These are the actual pre-approved words that the trust can include. This attorney added the word "comfort" to the list.

Upon review by the IRS, after the death of the second spouse, they determined that this word was not acceptable. This changed the trust completely, and the IRS hit the estate for $700,000 in additional taxes. The important point here is this was not determined until after the deaths of both of the spouses. As you can see, it was a little too late to make changes at this point.

This case was challenged in court and actually won. The court found that the spirit of the law was there, even if the proper wording was not. The bad news is that it was tied up in court for ten years! More bad news is that the ruling left the IRS free to pursue their argument in future cases.

As I mentioned previously, heirs cannot challenge the language of a trust. But in some cases, they can come very close. In this case, the husband and wife set up a trust which left all of their assets in seven equal shares to their seven children. Once again, it was a standard, normal trust.

A few years went by and the husband passed away. The wife went on as normal for a few more years. Suddenly, the wife was diagnosed with cancer. She began taking quite a bit of medication and underwent chemotherapy.

At this point, the wife started thinking about the inheritance she was leaving to her children. She was aware that some of her children were more successful than others. This became an issue of great concern to her. She began to feel guilty that she was giving money to some children who definitely did not need it, while other children needed it pretty badly.

The wife decided to amend the trust so that her less successful children received the bulk of her inheritance. She did this without informing the children, and it turned out to be a fairly large mistake.

When she eventually passed away, the trust documents were read to the children. As you can imagine, they took the children by surprise. The more successful children became somewhat disgruntled at being left out of the inheritance. They, of course, found an attorney that would represent them in court, and actually challenged their inheritance.

They were unable to actually challenge the wording of the trust. However, the amendment to the trust was not part of the original trust and could be challenged. Their argument was that their mother was not of sound mind as a result of all the drugs she had been taking. Doctors' opinions were brought in letters stating that the medication and treatment she had been undergoing would not affect her mental state.

The case never made it to court. Within the first year, the attorneys' fees had eaten away half of the $700,000 estate. The children dropped their lawsuit as a direct result of this. Once again, the only winners in this case were the lawyers. I would imagine that family gatherings have never been quite the same either.

This next case illustrates why it is so important to avoid those "cookie-cutter" trusts. It's too bad that the son became Jim's client after the damage was done. Like all the other stories, a lot of trouble could have been saved.

An older lady wanted to set up a trust for her estate. Her husband had already passed away and she only had one son. She shopped around and found the best deal she could on a trust. She found one that had been written by paralegals. They did not involve any lawyers, so they could keep the costs down.

In the trust, the lady made herself the trustee of her trust until she passed away. Then the duties of trustee would pass to her son. This was very simple and straightforward.

A few years passed and the lady's health deteriorated. She eventually became mentally incompetent and her son checked her into a nursing home. He needed to pay for the nursing home for his mother and the money was to come out of his mother's estate. He assumed the duties as trustee and went down to the bank to get the money. The bank reviewed the trust to make sure he was the proper trustee. He could not get to her money because he could not be the trustee. They argued that his mother was still alive and, according to the trust, she was still the trustee. There was no provision in the trust for mental incompetence.

The son's only recourse was to appeal in court. Eventually, through great expense and after much time, the court made him trustee. It sure would have been easier if the trust was set up correctly in the first place.

There must be language in the trust to change trustees. If a certain institution is named as trustee and another corporation buys out that institution, there has to be a way to change trustees to the new corporation. If not, this will result in more conflict and time in court.

These are just some very basic mistakes that can be seen in the "cookie-cutter" trusts that are so common today. If issues were more complicated, many more mistakes would be made. You really get what you pay for in estate planning. Look at who ultimately pays the price in each case: the heirs.

Mistake #5
Minimize Liability and Risk

Janet could have avoided the estate tax by making annual gifts of up to $10,000-$12,000 to family members. Norman and Margaret's decision to purchase long-term healthcare insurance reduced that risk to their financial security and saved the estate tens of thousands of dollars.

The trustee has many duties and responsibilities to the beneficiaries. The trustee is the protector of the assets. They are responsible for not only maintaining the current level of investments, but also ensuring that the investment will grow at a reasonable rate of return over the years. Maintaining the current level of assets is more difficult than you might think. There are many factors that can reduce your assets. In many cases, long-term sickness and taxes are the two biggest ways to quickly drain the savings which took a lifetime to acquire.

When properly planning for future finances involving trusts, there are three areas that need to be considered. These three areas involve: long-term sickness, taxes, and general lack of knowledge.

Long-term Sickness

It is estimated the average stay in a nursing home today costs roughly $5900 per month. As you can see, this can add up quickly over the course of a few years. If this was not planned for, then chances are there are other things overlooked in the financial plan as well. Fortunately, it is fairly easy to cover the risk of long-term sickness with long-term care insurance.

Long-term care insurance can be somewhat expensive. It is very important to look at the whole picture to determine the goals for this insurance. If you want it just to protect the current level of assets, then you only need enough to make up the difference between cost of care and current income.

Assume that the cost of long-term care is $5900 per month. If you subtract that from your social security income of $1000 per month, plus your earning of another $1000 per month in pension, your monthly insurance requirement is reduced to $3900. If you want to lower the premiums even further, you can up the deductible. Long-term care insurance is designed to cover your assets over the long term. Because of this, you can afford, in the short term, to make some payments to the facility out of your assets, in exchange for lower monthly rates on your insurance. The deductible in long-term care insurance is not measured in dollars, but in days. If you can afford 100 days to six months in a facility before insurance kicks in, you can significantly reduce monthly payments now. It is important to realize that this area of long-term sickness and insurance should not be ignored, because it can have a negative impact on your estate for your heirs.

Taxes

Did you know that estate taxes, taxes which are assessed on your estate after you and your spouse are gone, can reach up to 55% of your total assets? These taxes are due nine months after the death of the sole surviving spouse. They are due in cash to the IRS, payable by your heirs. If most of your estate is tied up in real estate, some of it will need to be sold in order to pay these taxes. So it may not even be possible to keep the family house in the family. It also includes selling other items that have increased in value over the years. For example, family heirlooms passed down for generations may not make it to the next generation, because the IRS may require them to be sold to pay the estate tax.

You may think that paying estate taxes are a necessary evil. But, in actuality, estate taxes can be considered a voluntary tax. Estate taxes are taxes for the unaware and can be very unnecessary. You can minimize the amount you pay and reduce the burden on your heirs through solid estate planning. Like long-term healthcare, this is an issue that must be planned before it's too late.

The first thing that must be done is to set up a good trust. Each individual gets a $625,000 exemption from the amount of estate taxes they must pay. If you and your spouse's estate is worth less than $625,000, you do not have much to worry about. If one spouse dies, the other still has her exemption to cover the assets from taxation.

If you have less than $1.25 million between the two of you, the process is a little more complicated, but still manageable. You must create an A-B trust. This will preserve your spouse's exemption after they die, so you can use it when you die to cover more assets. Because this procedure is a little more difficult, it should be prepared by a competent attorney (see Mistake #2).

The personal exemption is scheduled to increase to $3.5 million by the year 2009, which is good news for everybody. Your estate could easily grow by that much in that time, but be aware of some things first.

Lifetime Gift Tax Exemption: Your personal exemption will be increasing to the following amounts in the years stated:

2007	$2,000,000
2008	2,000,000
2009	3,500,000
2010	Estate Tax Repealed
2011	1,000,000

Keep in mind, when calculating your estate value, take EVERYTHING into consideration. Most people have no idea they were worth so much. They usually just calculate their liquid investments: stocks, bonds, money markets, savings and checking. They forget about houses, land, autos, heirlooms, jewelry and other items which cannot be spent and forgotten. It usually turns out they will owe more than originally thought.

One way to gradually reduce your estate, and consequently, your estate taxes, is to give gifts every year to those who are going to receive your inheritance. You can avoid paying a gift tax on these gifts by keeping them to $12,000 or less per person, per year. Furthermore, you can give to as many people as you like. This can reduce your estate over time, so you do not risk losing it right away. You can also control this gifting every year, by either increasing amounts (up to $12,000 per person) or decreasing them, as you see fit. This allows your heirs to benefit from their inheritance early, when they are more likely to need it, rather than later, when they might already have a comfortable estate of their own. Best of all, it allows you to experience the pleasure of giving while you are still around to enjoy it.

Plan carefully. You do not want to give everything away and later rely on others to take care of you in your old age. A good financial planner can help with this. There are several computer programs designed specifically to map out a course for people to reduce their estate through gifting and other options. A good financial planner should have access to a program that can design a sound plan, including several what-if scenarios that might require more finances that were overlooked.

Another way to cover estate taxes is through insurance. There are many different strategies to cover taxes through insurance. Once again, a good financial planner should be able to design a strategy for your specific situation. Insurance is actually a cheap, effective way to create wealth and eliminate taxes.

One type of insurance to consider is called a second-to-die, survivorship policy. It is very inexpensive, because it insures both spouses and does not pay benefits until both spouses die.

Let's assume you and your spouse have an estate valued at over $2 million. Let's also assume you went to a financial advisor and determined that if you and your spouse were to die right now, your estate taxes would come to roughly $400,000. This amount would be paid by your heirs. The heirs would receive this tax bill; there's no way around it.

Fortunately, if you bought a second-to-die, survivorship policy for a few thousand dollars per year to cover this $400,000 tax bill, your heirs would save far more than the amount you put into the insurance. They would be able to receive their entire inheritance without worrying about a large tax bill. They would also be able to keep the family house and any family heirlooms passed down from generations.

Keep in mind that this is only one example of many options available for estate planning. You must decide who you want to receive your estate—your heirs or the IRS. The choice is truly yours to make, and the lack of a decision and procrastination are decisions in themselves.

General Lack of Knowledge

There are many choices out there that most people just do not know about. People like to consider themselves good at picking stocks or mutual funds. But when you make more complex financial decisions, it is easy to make mistakes that can cost you in the long run. This is when you need to turn to others for help. There are people whose job it is to know the financial world and all of the options for individuals. These people are financial advisors. They make their living showing people how to not only make money, but also how to protect what they have from unforeseen disasters. These professionals should be sought out for such important decisions that estate planning requires. I found that people end up saving more money in the long run by consulting a professional than they do when they go it alone.

Example

A good example to show the importance of minimizing your liability and risk is the Sample case in the first chapter of this book. Janet took some actions that were able to give her a little more "peace of mind" by not having to worry about certain things. These actions will emphasize the importance of minimizing your liability and risk.

During the investigation by government officials, Janet received a call from a man claiming to be from the County of San Diego Area Agency on Aging. She thought this was another trick by Greg, but was not sure. At this point she was somewhat aware of Greg's greed, but not yet fully aware of his ruthlessness. The man said he was investigating her under the charges of "elder abuse" among other things. His department received three letters accusing her of this charge. Two of the letters were anonymous, and one was signed. He could not reveal who had signed the letter, but the charges were serious enough to warrant an investigation. He was calling to inform her she had been cleared of all charges.

Janet was, of course, relieved to hear this. She had not even known she was under investigation. She started talking to the man and asking questions about the investigation. He told her that if he had found enough evidence to support the charges, she could have gone to jail. She replied, "I don't think I would do very well in jail." She also could have lost all of the savings that she and her husband had worked so hard for all their lives. All this could have happened, and she had done nothing wrong.

Janet had escaped this attempt by Greg, but she needed to take action. Greg had been visiting Norman a few times and was stirring up trouble the whole time. Janet set some limitations on visitation for Norman. She said that anyone was more than welcome to visit him, but the nursing home had to get her prior approval. She would then need to be present during any visits. She made it clear to all the relatives that she was more than willing to meet them at the nursing home any time of day and any day of the week. All they had to do was call her. But not one relative even attempted to visit Norman after this. It just goes to show who actually cared about Norman, and who just cared about his money.

Another area where Janet had to reduce her liability was with Norman's house. It was on a one-acre lot with many fruit trees. There was quite a bit of upkeep involved, and Elsie was no longer there to do it. Janet called the insurance company to let them know the house was unoccupied. They thanked her for the information and told her she had thirty days to make it occupied or they would no longer insure it. This caused a mild panic. But Janet's son was just getting out of the Army, so she had him move in to take care of the place. The only mistake was that Janet was not charging him rent. She figured that to take care of a one acre lot was work enough, rather than charging rent. Of course, Greg did not feel this way and it became one of the issues in the lawsuit.

Norman had many fruit trees on his property. There were no fences around his yard, and the neighbors were free to come and pick any fruit they wanted at any time. The problem was most of the neighbors were older than Norman. There is a lot of liability when a ninety-year-old woman is trying to climb up on an overturned bucket to reach an orange. Janet had to make sure her son would pick any fruit the neighbors wanted at any time. She did not need a lawsuit from a neighbor.

Despite Norman's attitude towards nursing homes, the Samples minimized their liability was purchasing of long-term care insurance. Janet estimates that the total bill for Norman in the nursing home was $140,000. Norman had paid $250 a month for two years to receive this benefit. This was a small price to pay, and every case will not produce such a large benefit from such a small input. The whole purpose of insurance in the first place is protection. No one buys auto insurance hoping they will have a wreck, but it is there in case it happens. The reality is that if you are over the age of 65, you have a 43% chance of spending time in a nursing home (source: Worth, Feb.

1996). The average cost of a nursing home is $70,912 per year (source: *Genworth Financial 2007 Cost of Care Survey*). With the increase in age of life expectancies, there is a big possibility you, or someone you love, might end up in a nursing home. This event should be well planned for with proper insurance.

Mistake #6
Failure to Review Regularly

Janet fired her parents' financial advisor so there were no reviews of the trust from the legal, financial, and tax angles.

Acommon mistake among trustees is the failure to review the situation regularly. Life changes over time. So it is necessary to keep on top of the changes. If you review your estate and everything involved in its upkeep on a regular basis, you can make sure that you are almost always prepared for the many curves ahead.

The review process is divided into three critical areas: investment strategy, trust assets and advisors. All three of these areas need to be looked at on a regular basis.

Investment Strategy

When you look at your investment strategy, you need to look at two things—the short-term and the long-term. You should, at this point, already have a long-term plan written out and in place. You need to evaluate how your short-term investments are doing and determine if they are meeting your long-term goals. If you have a plan where a certain percentage of your assets are invested in stocks, while a certain percentage are in bonds, you need to make sure those percentages still hold true.

If stocks do well during a given period, and bonds remain flat, you will suddenly find yourself with a higher than desired percentage of stocks in your portfolio. With regular review, you can see and correct this problem. Or, perhaps you can change your short-term strategy to benefit your long-term goals. Either way, you will be making a decision, rather than have it made for you at a later time.

Another item to look at is the current tax law. If the law changes, it may have drastic effects on your assets and investments. These need to be monitored and changed as necessary. A good accountant will benefit you in this area. Your accountant can keep you informed of anything that will affect your situation. Also, a financial advisor should know how your investments will be affected by changes in the tax code and how to take advantage of these changes.

Trust Assets

It is important to look at everything in the trust and the total asset package of your estate every quarter. At this time, you can determine if you need to change any strategies that you have established, particularly if there are estate tax avoidance strategies. You need to see if your estate is growing and, if so, by how much. You need to also make sure that it will still carry you through your life expectancy. If anything needs to be changed, do it right away, to catch any potentially bad situations.

An important step is to document the reviews of your assets. Even if you change nothing, just initial and date each item, making notes of when you looked at them, and making sure to keep accurate records. This is important for future reference, so you can show you actually took the time to evaluate the progress of your plans. This is a good way, if you ever need to show in court that you actively managed the assets under your control.

There are times when your life will have dramatic changes. When these changes occur, you might not remember to make the necessary changes. Now this could have dramatic effects.

For example, let's assume you buy a life insurance policy and name your spouse as beneficiary. A few years go by and you get a divorce. Then you find the perfect new partner and are happily married. You forgot all about that insurance policy, so your first spouse is still the beneficiary when you pass away. Sadly, this is not a far-fetched scenario. It could happen and it often does. If you review your trust regularly, you can make the necessary changes as needed.

Advisors

Chances are, if you are happy with your advisors, you will still be happy over time. A periodic review does not usually cause sudden dissatisfaction with your advisor. Unhappiness with an advisor is usually triggered by an event. If this happens, you need to look at the total picture. Ask yourself if this person is giving you the advice that you need and carrying your desires out exactly as you have instructed. If your advisor is doing their job and you are still dissatisfied, you have to realize that your advisor might be giving you advice you might not want to hear, but need to hear.

One thing to keep in mind is that people change, including yourself. If your goals do not match those that you originally set, then look to your advisors for assistance in making changes. They may not be experienced in this new endeavor and should be up front and honest about their shortcomings. They might be able to recommend someone with more experience to help you.

Your advisors could also change. They might pass away or retire. Or they might lose what you originally saw in them. If this is the case, you need to remember that the trust is the most important thing here. You should do whatever is best for the trust in the long run. You might have to break a relationship with a long-time advisor. If this is necessary to benefit the trust, then it must be done. Your advisor will understand and will probably help you as much as possible.

The system I use for my clients provides a good way of reviewing regularly. My program allows trustees and beneficiaries to monitor progress on their investments. All beneficiaries and trustees receive a copy of a quarterly report. This report helps me explain any misunderstanding to them. The report breaks down the investments and shows the performance of each, whether they are out-performing or lagging the index. It is very clear and easy to understand. It shows the bases and capital gains for each account so everyone knows all the details. This is beneficial to both my clients and me. It allows communication between us. It also allows my clients to keep up on their account quarterly, so there are no surprises. Look for a similar program with your advisor, to help you keep up with your trust over time.

Be as active as you can in the trust's management, without getting bogged down in the day-to-day details. If you established a good plan and feel confident in your advisors, major changes should be unnecessary. You may have to tweak a few things here and there, but the original amount of work should pay off in the long run.

The most important thing about this chapter is to learn that things change over time. Everything must be reviewed periodically to ensure the original goals of the trust are being met. You must document everything you do when it comes to the trust. Even if you make no changes, you still must record that you looked everything over and took an active part in the management of the trust. You must maintain your confidence in your advisors by reviewing their services regularly. Do not be afraid to make changes to the long-term plans of the trust, if you feel the changes are necessary to achieve the goals you have set.

Mistake #7
Failure to Treat it Like a Business

Janet commingled some of the trust's assets and, while she spent the trust assets on Norman's care and welfare while he was alive, she didn't keep accurate records, resulting in a penalty of $35,000.

As a trustee, you need to think of yourself as a manager. You have a finite number of assets to manage, and your long-term goal is to make them grow. This is your business. Separate yourself from the beneficiaries, even if you are one. Think of them as shareholders—it is your job to maximize profits without taking on too much risk.

You are accountable to the beneficiaries for your actions. Whatever you do now, you may have to justify in a court of law in the future. You may be thinking, "No way, these are my relatives. They would never sue me. Blood is thicker than money." As you saw in the Sample case, nothing ends a relationship, even a blood relationship, more quickly than a dispute over money. I have seen it. My colleagues have seen it. It is not pretty. The important thing to realize is that it CAN happen. It is your job to cover yourself and do the best job possible.

If you take this very seriously, and treat the trust as if it were your business, you have a far greater chance of success. You are taking on a great liability, so you need to make sure you get good advice. I have already discussed the importance of proper advisors. If you were running a business, you would not try to do everything yourself. You cannot be expected to be an expert in accounting, law, and finances, on top of whatever your business is. In this situation, you would turn to good advisors to help you through the situations that were not your area of expertise.

Nowadays, there seem to be so many lawsuits that are unavoidable. It is true, some people are going to try to sue you no matter what you have done to protect yourself. It is your job to make good preparations so that a lawyer would not even want to take the case against you. Good advisors who went through similar situations can assist you to help you accomplish these preparations.

Organization is the most basic thing you can do to combat a potential lawsuit. If you keep accurate records of everything you do, have a good financial plan you follow, and review your plan regularly, you can head off most problems you might face in the future. This can take some time to organize, but, as you know, it will be well worth it in the long run.

Occasionally, my clients comment, "I seem to be doing all this work in order to benefit my siblings. I don't mean to seem greedy, but this is a lot to do for nothing." It is certainly within your right to charge a management fee for overseeing the trust. Believe it or not, it is actually encouraged, because it can mentally separate you from the fact that you are also a beneficiary. It is a lot of work, and you should be compensated for it. Obviously, you do not want to gouge the estate. Find out what a bank would charge to do the exact same thing. Then compare how much extra effort and personal attention you are putting into the care of the trust that the bank would not. This way it seems like the beneficiaries are getting a bargain. Chances are, you are more willing to do a good job, and take the time to do things right, if you are receiving some form of compensation. Do not be afraid of this, you deserve to be treated that way. You are a professional managing these assets as a business.

When you start thinking of your trust as a business, you will find it easier to make the decisions necessary to benefit the trust and the beneficiaries. It is their best interests you are looking out for. Keep that in mind above all else. If you keep them happy, then your rewards will benefit you in the long run.

Charles Marvyn

Charles Marvyn was an extremely successful man. He owned his own company, Marvyn, Inc., which he founded in the 50's. He built this company from nothing and did it by establishing loyalty from his employees. He set a policy early on that no matter what happened, he would never lay off or fire anyone at his company. As a result, his employees loved him and were willing to work for him for significantly less wages than most other companies in the same industry.

Charles disliked change. This quality showed up in his business and personal life. At his business, things were done and decisions were made based on what had been done in the past. There was not a lot of innovation, but fortunately John was in an industry that did not penalize for lack of ingenuity. All of his employees had been around for a long time, and they knew how to accomplish their tasks the same way every time. Eventually, everyone was afraid to make a decision that was against the grain.

I tried to work with Charles on his personal finances for years. He was worth a great deal of money, but refused to do any proper estate planning. The process went on for years: I would work on a good, solid plan for him, present it to him, and he would want to think about it for a while. This would go on and on and, as a result, no decision was his final decision. I tried for months to convince Charles he was creating a huge problem for his heirs. I worked with his son on a plan, but he was just as incapable of making a decision. I finally gave up, but kept in touch with the family in case they changed their minds. They never did.

About a year before he died, Charles sold his company. There were about 300 people in the company at the time. Unfortunately, Charles never set up a retirement plan for them and always paid them less than they were worth. Because he was loyal to them and never laid anyone off, they were loyal to him. When he sold the company, all his loyal employees got laid off with no 401(k) or other retirement plan in place to live off of. Most of them had not been able to save enough money over the years because of the low wages.

Here is where it gets interesting. Charles sold the company for about $3 million. Because of capital gains and other taxes, he paid the IRS $1.6 million of that money. If he would have planned for this properly, he could have given each employee about $65,000, instead of paying the IRS. His employees would have loved him forever. He would have been a legend. Instead, he was despised by his former workers. He left them out in the cold because he could not make a decision.

The funny thing is, the IRS is not done with Charles' money yet. When he died, his estate passed to his wife, who is now in a nursing home. They still have not set up any kind of estate plan. When she dies, the estate will write another check to the IRS for around $1 million. This is a terrible situation that would have been relatively simple to avoid.

Scenario

Throughout this book, I tried to explain the differences between mediocre planning and "super" planning. I talked about the advantages of "super" planning and why you should seek a team of advisors who can provide this for you. The following real-scenario highlights the benefits of planning. It shows it is possible to set your goals a little bit higher and be able to achieve those goals with proper planning. This couple was able to not only accomplish everything they set out to do, but also establish a legacy that will live on up to a hundred years after they are gone.

George and Rowena Rosen came to me for assistance with their estate planning. They managed to acquire enough assets that they felt it was necessary to properly plan what happened to everything after they passed on. They talked to each other about some specific goals and fears they each had about this. Then they decided they wanted to speak to a professional to help them formulate a plan.

George is 71 and Rowena is 69. They grew up during the Great Depression and had developed a "saver's mentality" as a result. This mentality helped them to acquire quite a large estate, but also kept them cautious about what they would invest their hard-earned money in. George also strongly felt he had paid his share of taxes throughout his life and thought it unfair that even when he died he would still have to pay them. He heard there might be ways to avoid estate taxes, but was unclear on how to go about it.

George and Rowena originally had two daughters. The oldest, Kim, was killed by a drunk driver at the age of 16. This had dramatically affected both George and Rowena's views on many things. For instance, they were very active in their support of anti-drunk driving causes. They also supported several charities that helped them through this tough time in their lives.

Their youngest daughter, Amy, is 38 and married to Jack, who is 42. They have three children, ages 2, 5 and 7. Jack is Amy's first husband; however, Jack was married before, but does not have any children by his first wife. Jack is an honest, hardworking individual and works as a fireman. Jill always stayed at home with the children. They are a very happy couple and keep in close contact with George and Rowena. The Rosens also think the world of their grandchildren.

George and Rowena attended several estate planning seminars before attending mine. Apparently, they liked what they saw in me because they asked for my assistance in planning their estate. They explained to me their situation through the course of several meetings. They shared with me their fears and goals for their assets.

The Rosen estate was made up of several different types of assets. The actual value came to about $1.9 million. It was fairly sizable, and certainly enough to have to worry about estate taxes. The estate breaks down as follows:

Asset	Approximate Value
· Home	$400,000
· IRA's	550,000
· Investments	450,000
· Rental Property	180,000
· Annuities	200,000
· Cash	30,000
· Insurance	75,000
Total	$ 1,885,000

The Rosens had already set up a trust with their lawyer and already had a financial planner and an accountant. Unfortunately, there was no communication between all the advisors. They had failed to use the Team Approach and, as a result, did not have an adequate estate plan. After my meetings with the Rosens, I did some calculations and determined that not only would their estate owe $543,000 in taxes upon their death, but it would also owe $232,500 in unpaid income taxes from the IRAs and annuities, for a total tax bill of $775,500. They knew some taxes would be due but were still somewhat surprised by this amount. I assured them there were ways to avoid this, as long as that was one of their goals.

I wanted to find out exactly what they wanted to happen after they died. So I explained to them that their trust needs to speak for them after they are gone, and that they needed to tell me everything. I first asked what the best thing they wanted that could happen with their money after they were gone. I wanted to try to reach this goal, even though they felt it could not be reached.

George and Rowena actually had several goals for their estate plan. Their first and foremost was to avoid paying those taxes. George was adamant about this, now more than ever. He just could not believe that this money that he had already paid taxes on was now going to be diminished even further.

The second goal was to make sure that Amy would be able to live a comfortable life from this inheritance. They were somewhat vague at this point and I needed more information. I wanted to see how comfortable they were with Jack. They said their relationship with him could not be any better. He was a hard worker, and a great husband and father. He called them regularly, just to see how they were doing. They thought Amy could not have picked a better husband. But they had one hesitation: George and Rowena were a little concerned Jack had been married before Amy. They were concerned about what would happen to their money if Jack and Amy decided to get a divorce. I told them that, as it is now, he would get half of it. As much as they loved Jack, this still made them uncomfortable. They really wanted Jill to be able to keep everything should the worst happen. After all, she was their daughter.

Their last major goal they had was to provide for some charities they had taken an interest in throughout their lives. When their daughter was struck by the drunk driver, she was taken to and cared for by Children's Hospital. They provided her daughter with what the Rosens felt was the best care possible. Since then, they had tried to help out the hospital whenever they could. The YMCA also was very supportive during this time. They wanted to provide for them as well. Rowena also was an active participant in Mothers Against Drunk Drivers (MADD). She still periodically volunteered her time there. She wanted to contribute some money to them. The Rosens also wanted to support the University of San Diego, the place where they first met. They had many happy memories of their times there and wanted to enable others to enjoy the school as much as they had.

Together they had come up with some fairly ambitious goals for their assets. I had a feeling they were not finished, though. So I asked them about their grandchildren. They replied that they definitely wanted to provide for them, but they just thought that came naturally through their aid to their daughter. I asked them what they wanted to do, if they could do anything, to help their grandchildren. They thought for a few minutes, and Rowena replied it would be nice to be able to make sure they could go to college. I smiled and told them I did not want to know what would be "nice", I wanted to know what they wanted to happen in a best-case scenario. They thought a little longer and said that, in addition to college, they would like to be able to allow them to purchase their first home. They felt this would be the largest expense their grandchildren would face in life, and they wanted to provide it for them. I clarified things by saying that they wanted to fully fund their grandchildren's college education and then be able to put a down payment on their first homes. Oh no, George quickly corrected me. Since I told them I wanted their best-case scenario, he wanted to PAY for a house for each of them.

I assured them I would give it my best attempt to accomplish all of their goals. They did not think it was going to be possible. They knew how much money they had and did not believe it was enough to do everything. They said they admired me for trying though.

—·—·—·—·—·—·—·—·—·—·—·—

The Plan

I worked on developing a good plan for the Rosens for several weeks. They had some lofty goals, but I thought I could create enough wealth for them to accomplish them, all the while still enabling them to live a full life. I did not want to jeopardize their current standard of living just to be able to provide for their heirs.

The first task was to protect their estate from anything which might erode it rapidly. I made a recommendation of long-term care insurance. George and Rowena each had the chances of 1 in 2 of spending their last few years in a nursing home. More than likely, one of them would have to be checked in to one. The expenses for this can really mount up, compared to the cost of the insurance. This would protect their assets for their heirs, and assure that they could stay in a nursing home as long as necessary.

The next step was to develop a plan for the heirs. I needed to maximize their inheritance, while ensuring George and Rowena they could still live in the manner to which they had become accustomed. I decided to set up a Children's/Grandchildren's Trust. This trust would protect its assets from taxation and still provide benefits to all the heirs. It would also enable George and Rowena to set up definite guidelines for what would happen to their money.

I funded the trust with an insurance policy, more specifically, a second-to-die policy on George and Rowena. This meant the policy would not pay a death benefit until both of them died. It also was a lot cheaper than purchasing two policies for them. I figured they would need a $3.5 million policy to accomplish all of their goals.

The policy premiums were paid by annuitizing the annuity over a five-year period. This would provide them with annual payments of roughly $40,000. They would combine this with an annual withdrawal from their IRAs of $40,000, for a total of $80,000. They would divide this among their daughter and their three grandchildren by gifting $20,000 to each of them. This would be free of any gift taxes because of the annual $10,000 gift tax exclusion. These $20,000 gifts would then be used to pay for the insurance. This would keep it out of their estate and still create a huge inheritance for their heirs.

Once the Rosens both pass away, the trust receives the $3.5 million. It then controls the money. Immediately, $500,000 is paid out to the charities – $125,000 to each. The remaining $3 million remains in the trust. This money is invested for the beneficiaries at a modest 10% rate of return on the investments within the portfolio.

While Amy is alive, she receives half of the interest generated by this $3 million, or $150,000. The other half remains in the trust to allow it to grow to and compensate for inflation. Amy is restricted from receiving any of the principal, except in certain instances. Once her children reach a certain age, she is able to distribute some of the principal to them to pay for college and their first home.

When Amy eventually dies, the trust splits into three entities—one for each of the grandchildren. This provides a minimum of $1 million to each grandchild. However, this money is to be distributed in five payments throughout their lives. The first payment is made at age 25, the next at 35, and so on every ten years until the age of 65, when the trust will pay out the remainder of its assets and dissolves.

This arrangement will basically provide for Amy for her entire life, as well as for her children for most of their lives. They will be able to do whatever they wish in life, pursuing any career that interests them, and not being limited by finances. It is an amazing concept and they will owe it all to their grandparents.

George and Rowena were very pleased with my plan. They implemented it over the next several weeks and have now established a legacy that will live on for many years after they are gone. They were able to accomplish all of their goals, and some they had not even considered. It was not extremely difficult, because they realized they needed professional help. I have handled many cases very similar to the Rosens, so I was able to draw on quite a bit of experience. If they had tried to develop a plan as elaborate as this on their own, I doubt they would have been able. It is nothing to be ashamed of, this is just not their area of expertise.

When it comes to estate planning, you must decide for yourself what type of planning you want to do. Some people are content to leave their heirs whatever they get. They feel that something is better than nothing. These types of people have no interest in "super" planning. They also have no need for it. This type of planning is only for those who want to maximize what their heirs receive, while minimizing what the government receives. It all depends on your outlook.

Glossary

Annuity & Life Insurance Terms

ANNUITANT

The person(s) who receives the income from an annuity contract. Usually the owner of the contract or his or her spouse.

ANNUITIZATION

The conversion of the account balance of a deferred annuity contract to income payments.

ANNUITY

A life insurance product that pays periodic income benefits for a specific period of time or over the course of the annuitant's lifetime. There are two basic types of annuities: deferred and immediate: Deferred annuities allow assets to grow tax deferred over time before being converted to payments to the annuitant. Immediate annuities allow payments to begin within about a year of purchase.

ANNUITY ACCUMULATION PHASE OR PERIOD

The period during which the owner of a deferred annuity makes payments to build up assets.

ANNUITY ADMINISTRATIVE CHARGES

Covers the cost of customer services for owners of variable annuities.

ANNUITY BENEFICIARY

In certain types of annuities, a person who receives annuity contract payments if the annuity owner or annuitant dies while payments are still due.

ANNUITY CONTRACT

An agreement similar to an insurance policy for other insurance products such as auto insurance.

ANNUITY CONTRACT OWNER

The person or entity that purchases an annuity and has all rights to the contract. Usually, but not always, the annuitant (the person who receives incomes from the contract).

ANNUITY DEATH BENEFITS

The guarantee that if an annuity contract owner dies before annuitization (the switchover from the savings to the payment phase) the beneficiary will receive the value of the annuity that is due.

ANNUITY INSURANCE CHARGES

Covers administrative and mortality and expense risk costs.

ANNUITY INVESTMENT MANAGEMENT FEE

The fee paid for the management of variable annuity invested assets.

ANNUITY ISSUER

The insurance company that issues the annuity.

CASH SURRENDER VALUE

The equity amount available to the owner of a life insurance policy should he or she decide it is no longer wanted. Calculated separately from the legal reserve.

CASH VALUE

The equity amount available to the policy owner when a life insurance policy is surrendered to the company, or the amount upon which the total available for a policy loan is determined. During the early policy years in a traditional whole life policy, the cash value is the reserve less a surrender charge; in the later policy years, the cash surrender value usually equals or closely approximates the reserve value.

CONTINGENT BENEFICIARY

Beneficiary of a life insurance or annuity policy who is entitled to receive the policy proceeds on the insured's death if the primary beneficiary dies before the insured; or the beneficiary who receives the remaining payments if the primary beneficiary dies before receiving the guaranteed number of payments.

FIXED ANNUITY

An annuity that guarantees a specific rate of return. In the case of a deferred annuity, a minimum rate of interest is guaranteed during the savings phase. During the payment phase, a fixed amount of income, paid on a regular schedule, is guaranteed.

FREE-LOOK PERIOD

A period of up to one month during which the purchaser of an annuity can cancel the contract with no penalty. Rules vary by state.

Guarantee Period
Period during which the level of interest specified under a fixed annuity is guaranteed.

Guaranteed Death Benefit
Basic death benefits guaranteed under variable annuity contracts.

Guaranteed Living Benefit
A guarantee in a variable annuity that a certain level of annuity payment will be maintained. Serves as a protection against investment risks. Several types exist.

Joint and Survivor Annuity
An annuity with two annuitants, usually spouses. Payments continue until the death of the longest living of the two.

Mortality and Expense (M & E) Risk Charge
A fee that covers such annuity contract guarantees as death benefits.

Planned Premium
The premium amount specified by the policy owner as the amounts intended to be paid at fixed intervals over a specified period of time. Premiums may be paid on a monthly, quarterly, semi-annual or annual basis. If policy values are adequate, the specified premium need not be paid, and can be changed at any time. Within limits, premium payments that are more or less than the specified premium amount may be permitted.

Policy Basis
The policy basis represents the policy owner's investment in the policy. Policy basis is used in determining the taxable portion of a policy distribution when a taxable event occurs. For example, the portion of the surrender proceeds or withdrawal distribution that exceeds the policy basis is reported as taxable income (gain).

Policy Loan
A loan made by an insurance company to a policyholder on the security of the cash value of the policy.

Prospectus
Legal document providing detailed information about variable annuity or life insurance contracts. Must be offered to each prospective buyer.

Surrender Charge
A charge for withdrawals from an annuity or life insurance contract before a designated surrender charge period..

TERM INSURANCE

Type of life insurance that provides temporary protection for a specified number of years

UNDERWRITING

Examining, accepting, or rejecting insurance risks and classifying the ones that are accepted, in order to charge appropriate premiums for them.

UNIVERSAL LIFE INSURANCE

A flexible premium policy that combines protection against premature death with a type of savings vehicle, known as a cash value account, that typically earns a money market rate of interest. Death benefits can be changed during the life of the policy within limits, generally subject to a medical examination. Once funds accumulate in the cash value account, the premium can be paid at any time but the policy will lapse if there isn't enough money to cover annual mortality charges and administrative costs.

VARIABLE ANNUITY

An annuity whose contract value or income payments vary according to the performance of the stocks, bonds and other investments selected by the contract owner.

VARIABLE LIFE INSURANCE

A policy that combines protection against premature death with a savings account that can be invested in stocks, bonds, and money market mutual funds at the policyholder's discretion.

WHOLE LIFE INSURANCE

The oldest kind of cash value life insurance that combines protection against premature death with a savings account. Premiums are fixed and guaranteed and remain level throughout the policy's lifetime.

Estate Planning Terms

A/B TRUST

A type of Revocable Living Trust used by married couples. In this type of living trust, two trusts (trust A and trust B) are created at the time the first spouse dies. By dividing the couple's estate into two trusts at the first death, each spouse can pass the maximum amount of property allowed to avoid federal estate taxes. One trust, usually trust A, is often referred to as the marital deduction trust and the other trust, usually trust B, is often referred to as the shelter trust.

ADMINISTRATION

The care and management of an estate by an executor, an administrator, a trustee, or a guardian.

ADMINISTRATOR/EXECUTOR

A person appointed by the court to administer (i.e. manage or take charge of) the assets and liabilities of a decedent. If the person performing these services is named by the decedent's will, he is designated as the executor of the estate.

ADVANCE DIRECTIVES

Written instructions, such as a living will or durable power of attorney for health care, which guides care when an individual is terminally ill or incapacitated and unable to communicate his/her desires.

ANNUAL GIFT EXCLUSION

The amount of property the IRS allows a person to gift to another person during a calendar year before a gift tax is assessed and/ or a gift tax return must be filed. The amount is increased periodically. There is no limit to the number of people you can give gifts to which qualify for the annual exclusion. To qualify for the annual exclusion, the gift must be one that a recipient can enjoy immediately and have full control over.

ASSETS

Property owned, in this case by an insurance company, including stocks, bonds, and real estate. Insurance accounting is concerned with solvency and the ability to pay claims. State insurance laws therefore require a conservative valuation of assets, prohibiting insurance companies from listing assets on their balance sheets whose values are uncertain, such as furniture, fixtures, debit balances, and accounts receivable that are more than 90 days past due. (See Admitted assets)

BENEFICIARY

An individual, institution, trustee or estate which receives, or may become eligible to receive, benefits under a will, insurance policy, retirement plan, annuity, trust, or other contract.

BY-PASS TRUST

An estate planning device (also called a credit shelter trust, family trust, or B trust in "AB" plans where the A trust funds for the marital deduction) used to minimize the combined estate taxes payable by spouses whereby, at the death of the first spouse, the estate is divided into two parts and one part is placed in trust usually to benefit the surviving spouse without being taxed at the surviving spouse's death, while the other part passes outright to the surviving spouse or is placed in a marital deduction trust. A by-pass trust permits a maximum of $2,000,000 transfer to heirs of the spouses on an estate tax-free basis under the unified gift and estate tax credits as they exist in 2007.

CHARITABLE GIFT ANNUITY

An arrangement whereby the donor makes a gift to charity and receives back a guaranteed lifetime (or joint lifetime) income based on the age(s) of the annuitant(s).

CHARITABLE LEAD TRUST

An arrangement whereby the charity receives an income from a trust for a period of years, then the remainder is paid to non-charitable beneficiaries (generally either the donor or his or her heirs).

CHARITABLE REMAINDER ANNUITY TRUST

A charitable trust arrangement whereby the donor or other beneficiary is paid annually an income of a fixed amount of at least 5% but not more than 50% of the initial fair market value of property placed in the trust, for life or for a period of up to 20 years; one or more qualified charitable organizations must be named to receive the remainder interest upon the death of the donor or other income beneficiaries, and the value of the charitable remainder interest must be at least 10% of the net fair market value of all property transferred to the trust, as determined at the time of the transfer.

CHARITABLE REMAINDER TRUST

An arrangement wherein the remainder interest goes to a legal charity upon the termination or failure of a prior interest.

CHARITABLE REMAINDER UNITRUST

A charitable trust arrangement whereby the donor or other beneficiary is paid annually an income of a fixed percentage of at least 5% but not more than 50% of the annually revalued trust assets, for life or for a period of up to 20 years; one or more qualified charitable organizations must be named to receive the remainder interest upon the death of the donor or other income beneficiaries, and the value of the charitable remainder interest must be at least 10% of the net fair market value of all property transferred to the trust, as determined at the time of the transfer.

CHILDREN'S TRUST

An irrevocable trust funded through gifts using either the $12,000 per person annual gift exemption or by using all or a portion of the unified credit exclusion of $2,000,000 per person or $4,000,000 per couple. The trust is for the benefit of the grantors' heirs and is set up to continue benefiting the family for multiple generations. Also commonly referred to as a Dynasty Trust.

CONSERVATOR

Generally, an individual or a trust institution appointed by a court to care for property; specifically, an individual or a trust institution appointed by a court to care for and manage the property of an incompetent, in much the same way as that in which a guardian cares for and manages the property of a ward.

DECEDENT

The person who has died.

DONOR

A person who makes a gift. The person setting up a trust can be called donor, trustor, grantor, or settlor.

DURABLE POWER OF ATTORNEY

A written legal document which allows one person (the principal) to authorize another person (the attorney-in-fact or agent) to act on his or her behalf with respect to specified types of property, and which may remain in effect during a subsequent disability or incompetency of the principal.

DURABLE POWER OF ATTORNEY FOR HEALTH CARE

A written legal document which grants decision-making powers related to health care to an agent; generally provides for removal of a physician, the right to have the incompetent patient discharged against medical advice, the right to medical records, and the right to have the patient moved or to engage other treatment.

ESTATE

Everything of value (all property) that a person owns while living or at the time of death.

ESTATE PLANNING

Process designed to conserve estate assets before and after death, distribute property according to the individual's wishes, minimize federal estate and state inheritance taxes, provide estate liquidity to meet costs of estate settlement, and provide for the family's financial needs.

ESTATE TAX

A tax imposed on the transfer of property from a decedent to his or her heirs, legatees or devisees.

ESTATE PLANNING

Process designed to conserve estate assets before and after death, distribute property according to the individual's wishes, minimize federal estate and state inheritance taxes, provide estate liquidity to meet costs of estate settlement, and provide for the family's financial needs.

Estate Tax
A tax imposed on the transfer of property from a decedent to his or her heirs, legatees or devisees.

Fiduciary
A person in the position of great trust and responsibility, such as the executor of a will or the trustee of a trust.

General Power of Appointment
A power of the donee (the one who is given the power) to pass on an interest in property to whomever he pleases, including himself or his estate.

Generation Skipping Transfer (GST)
A transfer of property, usually in trust, that is designed to provide benefits for beneficiaries who are two or more generations younger than the generation of the grantor.

Generation Skipping Transfer Tax (GST)
A transfer tax generally assessed on transfers to grandchildren, great grandchildren and others who are at least two generations younger than the donor.

Generation Skipping Transfer Tax Exemption
An exemption from generation-skipping tax for transfers by an individual either during life or at death.

Generation Skipping Trust
Any trust having beneficiaries who belong to two or more generations younger than the grantor.

Gift
A voluntary transfer of property for which nothing of value is received in return. If the Internal Revenue Service is to recognize a transfer as a gift, the donor(s) must unconditionally transfer all title and control of the property to the recipient(s) at the time the gift is given.

Gifting
A means of implementation of an estate plan through gifts to intended successors in the ownership of assets owned by the person(s) making the gifts.

Grantee
A person to whom property is transferred by deed or to whom property rights are granted by means of a trust instrument or some other document.

GRANTOR

The person who establishes the trust. Also called the creator, settlor, donor or trustor.

GROSS ESTATE

The total value of all property in which a deceased had an interest. This must be included in his or her estate for federal tax purposes.

HEIR

A person entitled by law to inherit part or all of the estate of an ancestor who died without leaving a valid will.

INCIDENTS OF OWNERSHIP

Includes a variety of rights and powers that an insured decedent may have held over a life insurance policy; the possession of one or more of these incidents of ownership within three years of death will bring the policy proceeds into the insured's gross estate.

INCOME BENEFICIARY

The beneficiary of a trust who is entitled to receive the income from it.

IRREVOCABLE LIFE INSURANCE TRUST

An irrevocable trust established to own an insurance policy or policies and thereby prevent them from being included in the insured's estate. This trust is usually set up to distribute to the beneficiaries upon the death of the insureds for the payment of estate taxes.

IRREVOCABLE TRUST

A trust that cannot be changed or terminated after it is established.

LIVING TRUST

A written legal document into which you place all of your property, with instructions for its management and distribution upon your disability or death.

MARITAL DEDUCTION

A deduction allowing for the unlimited transfer of any or all property from one spouse to the other generally free of estate and gift tax.

POUR OVER WILL

This is a Will used to transfer (pour over) into a trust any property that is left in a person's estate after death.

POWER OF APPOINTMENT

A right given to another in a written instrument, such as a will or trust, that allows the other to decide how to distribute your property. The power of appointment is "general" if it places no restrictions on who the distributees may be. A power is "limited" or "special" if it limits the eventual distributee.

POWER OF ATTORNEY

A written legal document that gives an individual the authority to act for another. If the authority is to act for the principal in all matters, it is a general power of attorney. If the authority granted is limited to certain specified things, it is a special power of attorney. If the authority granted survives the disability of the principal, it is a durable power of attorney.

PRIMARY BENEFICIARY

Beneficiary of a life insurance policy who is first entitled to receive the policy proceeds on the insured's death.

PROBATE

A court procedure for settling the personal affairs of a decedent by formally proving the validity of a will and establishing the legal transfer of property to beneficiaries, or appointing an administrator and supervising the legal transfer of property to heirs if there is no valid will.

PRUDENT MAN RULE

An investment standard. In some states, the law requires that a fiduciary, such as a trustee, may invest the trust's or fund's money only in a list of securities designated by the state. In other states, the trustee may invest in a security if it is one which a prudent man of discretion and intelligence, who is seeking a reasonable income and preservation of capital, would buy.

PRUDENT PERSON

A person who acts cautiously in the handling of assets. See Prudent Man Rule.

REGISTERED INVESTMENT ADVISOR

An individual or firm able to fully manage a portfolio for an "RIA" client under the Prudent Investor Act.

REVOCABLE TRUST

A trust that can be changed after it is established. Assets can be added or removed from the corpus of the trust, the beneficiary(ies) can be changed, and other changes, including termination of the trust, are allowed.

State Death or Inheritance Taxes

The tax imposed by the state in which you live and/or where your property is located, if different, on the transfer of that property to another at your death.

Step Up In Basis

A decedent's capital gains property that passes to others escaping capital gains tax when sold by the person who inherits the property. Persons inheriting capital gains property receive the property at date-of-death fair market value. In effect, the basis in this property is deemed to be "stepped up" and does not reflect the decedent's original cost basis for determining applicable capital gains tax on the sale of the property.

Taxable Estate

The portion of an estate that is subject to federal estate taxes or state death taxes. Technically, all of an estate is subject to federal estate taxes, but because of the unified credit, only estates with a value over the exemption equivalent amount actually have to pay any estate taxes (see Appendix 1). Therefore, it is common to refer to an estate with a value over the exemption equivalent amount as a taxable estate and an estate with a value under the exemption equivalent amount as a nontaxable estate.

Tenants In Common

A form of asset ownership in which two or more persons have an undivided interest in the asset and the ownership shares are not required to be equal.

Trust

A legal arrangement in which an individual (the trustor) gives fiduciary control of property to a person or institution (the trustee) for the benefit of beneficiaries.

Trust Declaration or Trust Instrument

A document defining the nature and duration of the trust, the powers of the trustee, and identifying the trust's beneficiary(ies).

Trustee

An individual or organization which holds or manages and invests assets for the benefit of another.

Unified Tax Credit

Tax credit that can be used to reduce the amount of the federal estate or gift tax.

Uniform Gifts (Transfers) To Minors Act (UGMA or UTMA)

A method to hold property for the benefit of a minor, which is similar to a trust but the rules are governed by state law.

WILL

A person's written declaration of desires for disposal of his or her property after death.

Financial Planning Terms

401(K) PLAN

A qualified profit sharing or stock bonus plan under which plan participants have an option to put money into the plan or receive the same amount as taxable cash compensation. Amounts contributed to the plan are not taxable to the participants until withdrawn. Generally funded entirely or in part through salary reductions elected by employees. Salary reductions are subject to an annual limit.

403(B) PLAN

A tax-deferred annuity retirement plan available to employees of public schools and certain nonprofit organizations.

457 PLAN

A plan which provides an exclusion from gross income for a certain portion of salary deferred by a participant under the plan of a state or local government, a tax-exempt organization (excluding churches), or of an independent contractor of such government or organization (e.g., a physician providing independent services to a hospital).

BEFORE-TAX EARNINGS

A taxpayer's gross income from salary, commissions, sales, fees, etc., before deductions for federal, state or other income taxes.

BOND

A security that obligates the issuer to pay interest at specified intervals and to repay the principal amount of the loan at maturity. In insurance, a form of suretyship. Bonds of various types guarantee a payment or a reimbursement for financial losses resulting from dishonesty, failure to perform and other acts.

CAPITAL GAIN OR CAPITAL LOSS

The profit or loss from the sale of a capital asset.

COST BASIS

The owner's cost of an asset for income and estate tax purposes as determined under the Internal Revenue Code and IRS regulations.

Defined Benefit Plan

A retirement plan under which pension benefits are fixed in advance by a formula based generally on years of service to the company multiplied by a specific percentage of wages, usually average earnings over that period or highest average earnings over the final years with the company.

Defined Contribution Plan

An employee benefit plan under which the employer sets up benefit accounts and contributions are made to it by the employer and by the employee. The employer usually matches the employee's contribution up to a stated limit.

Deferred Compensation Plan

A plan in which the executive elects to defer compensation into an account in the expectation of receiving the deferrals plus earnings at retirement; may involve company contributions.

DJ Industrial Average - 30 Industrial: Prepared and published by Dow Jones & Co.

It's one of the oldest and most widely quoted of all the market indicators. The Dow Jones Industrial Average is comprised of 30 stocks that are major factors in their industries, and widely held by individuals and institutional investors.

These 30 stocks represent about a fifth of the $8 trillion-plus market value of all U.S. stocks and about a fourth of the value of stocks listed on the New York Stock Exchange.

Equity/Stock

In investments, the ownership interest of shareholders. In a corporation, stocks as opposed to bonds.

Fair Market Value

The price at which an item can be sold at the present time between two unrelated people, neither under compulsion to buy or sell.

Individual Retirement Account (IRA)

A tax-deferred retirement account for an individual that can be established by a person with earned income. Earnings accumulate tax-deferred until the funds are withdrawn, beginning at age 59 ½ or later (or earlier, with a 10% penalty).

Investment Gain/Loss

The total increase or decrease in account value as a result of investment division performance during the policy year.

Liability

A financial obligation, debt, claim, or potential loss.

MUTUAL FUND

A popular expression for an open-end investment company. A company that sells shares to the public, pools the proceeds, and invests in different types of securities. It thus offers the small investor the advantages of diversification and reduction of investment risk. The company is obligated to redeem or repurchase its shares on request.

NASDAQ

The NASDAQ Composite Index measures all NASDAQ domestic and non-U.S. based common stocks listed on The NASDAQ Stock Market. The Index is market-value weighted. This means that each company's security affects the Index in proportion to its market value. The market value, the last sale price multiplied by total shares outstanding, is calculated throughout the trading day, and is related to the total value of the Index.

PREFERRED STOCKS

Stock shares that pay dividends or interest at a fixed rate. A preferred stock security is a hybrid between a stock and a bond. Most preferred stocks are structured as "baby bonds" and therefore pay interest income. Preferred stock enjoys prior claim to company assets in the event of bankruptcy versus common stock holders. Preferred stock does not usually carry voting rights, however.

QUALIFIED PLAN

Plans that qualify for favorable tax treatment under the Internal Revenue Code, and are subject to restrictive rules and extensive regulations. Qualified plans are secured by a trust, as opposed to a non-qualified plan.

REAL ESTATE INVESTMENT TRUST (REIT)

An investment trust that owns and manages a pool of commercial properties and mortgages and other real estate assets.

SECURITIES

Literally, things given, deposited, or pledged to assure the fulfillment of an obligation. In this narrow sense, a mortgage is a security; but the term is now generally used in a broader sense to include stocks as well as bonds, notes, and other evidences of indebtedness.

SIMPLIFIED EMPLOYEE PENSION (SEP) IRA

A retirement program for self-employed people or owners of small companies allowing them to defer taxes on investments intended for retirement

STANDARD AND POORS

Analysts for stocks, bonds etc. run the well known "500" index of the largest 500 (S&P) companies in the United States.

TREASURY BILLS

US government securities that are usually issued with maturities of 3, 6, or 12 months.

TREASURY BONDS

US government securities that mature in 10 to 30 years.

TREASURY NOTES

US government securities that mature in 2 to 10 years.

VOLATILITY

Risk that an investment may go up or down in value. Generally presented in the form of the result of a computation known as standard deviation. A government securities mutual fund may have a standard deviation of 2. An S&P 500 stock fund may have a standard deviation of 20.

YIELD

Generally applied to a bond, where it reflects the interest paid in relation to the current value of the bond.

today's
TRUSTEEONLINE

Learn the Best Strategies of Estate Planning and Avoid the Common Mistakes that Can Sink Your Financial Dreams and Tear Apart Your Family

IS *TODAY'S TRUSTEE ONLINE* FOR YOU?
IF YOU:

- HAVE ESTABLISHED A TRUST,
- HAVE BEEN NAMED AS A BENEFICIARY,
- ARE A TRUSTEE, OR HAVE BEEN ASKED TO BE ONE,
- ARE LOOKING FOR THE BEST ESTATE PLANNING STRATEGIES

—the answer is ABSOLUTELY YES!

There's no other resource like this for trust grantors, trustees, and beneficiaries to help you work through the challenges you are sure to face.

It's a publication that has long-term value. You'll hold on to it and go back over the information often because it's practical, timely, and high value.

And it's **FREE**.

Each issue of Today's Trustee brings you practical, unbiased information from leading authorities in areas such as:

• **Trustee Responsibilities:** Should you be a trustee? Do you have the time and experience to handle all of the duties? Are you aware of your liabilities as a trustee? Are you prepared to handle conflicts with family members when there's miscommunication and resentment?

• **Estate Planning:** The pros and cons of hiring a financial advisor and how do you pick the right one to help you with your estate plans?

• **Tax Issues:** Do you know what the latest tax legislation is and how it will affect your estate plan?

- **Investing:** What are the best investments for you and your future? What's working for someone else may be the worst thing for you.
- **Legal Matters:** Are you familiar with the *Uniform Prudent Investor Act* (UPIA) that governs the standards for managing a trust? Do you know the legal consequences of not following the UPIA statutes?
- **Managed Care:** What's involved in moving your mom or dad into managed care, especially if they don't what to go? What's the right kind of long term care insurance to own? When's the best time to get it?
- **Multi-generational Planning:** Do you know the right strategies for including 1st, 2nd, and 3rd generations in your living trust?
- **Advanced Strategies:** Do you want unbiased, independent estate solutions that utilize a large array of financial companies, top quality products and investment opportunities?

In addition each issue highlights true accounts of people who've experienced first hand, the good, the bad, and the ugly of estate planning. Through these sometimes traumatic and heart wrenching stories you'll learn how to avoid costly mistakes-before they happen to you.

The unfortunate reality is that too many people, when faced with having to confront family conflicts and make sense of the financial and legal complexities of estate planning, procrastinate and in many cases... do nothing. This lack of action often snowballs into a crisis.

The purpose of *TODAY'S TRUSTEE* is to empower you with the knowledge and tools you need to take control of your financial future and create the lifestyle you desire for yourself and your family.

For your FREE subscription go to
www.todaystrustee.com or call toll free
1-888-905-TRUSTEE (8787)

ADVANCED TRUSTEE STRATEGIES

Recommended Trustee and Estate Planning Seminars

ATS (Advanced Trustee Strategies) Financial Services provides seminars for anyone involved with a living trust. In the last 13 years they have presented over 494 seminars and workshops primarily in San Diego and the San Francisco Bay Area. Because they are an independent company they are free to present only the strategies that are best for you.

These seminars are for educational purposes only and not used as a venue for selling investment products and services.

ATS is committed to providing high quality, interesting, and useful information to its clients, friends, and the public. Their seminar format is conducive to learning. This helps ensure that you can use the information presented.

Sandeep Varma, author and the creative mind and backbone of ATS, developed their signature seminar, *"The Seven Biggest Mistakes Trustees Often Make"* based on his experience with a client family. He witnessed, firsthand, how greed, miscommunication, and bad legal and financial advice caused his clients' estate plans and family relationships to unravel. All of it was preventable. Unfortunately, the circumstances are all too familiar. The seminar was developed to help people to avoid these common mistakes.

We found that most people have only laid a foundation for estate planning by establishing a living trust. Most haven't built upon that foundation. This is because their advisors don't educate them about the many strategies available to them. Or they have misconceptions about some of the strategies, financial services, and products.

For this reason ATS developed Advanced Trustee Workshops as a "next step" for seminar attendees.

For more information about these seminars visit:
www.atsfinancial.com
or call 1-888-446-8275.

Recommended Fiduciaries

ATHERTON TRUST COMPANY

A full range of trustee services for you including: trust administration, investments in securities, real estate and collectibles, tax strategy and accounting for trust assets, and for generations of beneficiaries, financial and estate planning, record keeping and reporting to beneficiaries and management of trust assets including real estate.

Their concept is simple: A one stop, comprehensive service company where you can get all of the institutional level services you need, at a cost you can afford.

They recognize that every client and family is different; they tailor their services to meet your individual needs, as compared to large institutions that provide a more structured or limited set of trustee services.

Kraig Kast, Atherton Trust's CEO, leads a national team of over 300 trust and wealth management professionals. In his 25 year career as an advisor and investor, Kraig has been involved in investment transactions with an asset value in excess of $900 million and has personally negotiated contracts ranging from $50,000 to $250 million.

Atherton Trust
303 Twin Dolphin Drive, Sixth Floor
Redwood Shores, CA 94065

Telephone: 650-341-4480
Facsimile: 650-341-4417
Website: www.athertontrust.com
Email: information@athertontrust.com